HOW TO PLAY
PIANO

Pamela D. Pike, PhD, NCTM

THE
GREAT
COURSES

Published by

THE GREAT COURSES

Corporate Headquarters

4840 Westfields Boulevard | Suite 500 | Chantilly, Virginia | 20151-2299

[PHONE] 1.800.832.2412 | [FAX] 703.378.3819 | [WEB] www.thegreatcourses.com

Pamela D. Pike, PhD, NCTM

Aloysia Landry Barineau Professor of Piano Pedagogy
Louisiana State University

Pamela D. Pike is the Aloysia Landry Barineau Professor of Piano Pedagogy at Louisiana State University (LSU), where she coordinates the group piano and piano pedagogy programs. She earned a bachelor of music with honors in Piano Performance from The University of Western Ontario, a master of music in Piano Pedagogy and Music History from Southern Illinois University, and a PhD in Music Education and Piano Pedagogy from the University of Oklahoma.

Dr. Pike is a Nationally Certified Teacher of Music (NCTM) and has extensive experience teaching piano to students of all ages, both privately and in group settings. She founded the Third-Age Piano Class, a group in Little Rock, Arkansas, for senior citizens to study piano and make music. The program has become a model for successful community engagement. In addition to teaching piano, Dr. Pike is dedicated to helping pedagogy students develop the skills necessary to become successful piano teachers. Graduates of the LSU piano pedagogy program work in colleges and private studios throughout the United States and on four continents.

Dr. Pike is the author of the book *Dynamic Group-Piano Teaching: Transforming Group Theory into Teaching Practice* as well as the book chapter "Internships" in *High-Impact Practices in Online Education*. She also has contributed chapters to pedagogical publications by The Royal Conservatory of Music in Toronto, Ontario, on topics such as developing student artistry at the intermediate levels and developing advanced technical skills.

Additionally, Dr. Pike has published more than three dozen scholarly articles in peer-reviewed journals, including the *International Journal of Music Education; Psychology of Music; Music Education Research;* the *Journal of Music, Technology & Education;* the *Journal of Music Teacher Education; Problems in Music Pedagogy; Clavier Companion; Keyboard Companion; College Music Symposium;* the *MTNA e-Journal;* and *American Music Teacher.* Dr. Pike won the Music Teachers National Association's Article of the Year Award for her article "Sight-Reading Strategies for the Beginning and Intermediate Piano Student." She is also on the editorial committee of the *MTNA e-Journal* and the editorial board of the *Journal of Music, Technology & Education,* and she is the editor in chief and chief content director of *Clavier Companion.*

Dr. Pike serves as a commissioner and chair for the International Society for Music Education's Commission on the Education of the Professional Musician. She also chairs the College Music Society's Committee on Engagement with Higher Education, is a board member of Yamaha's Disklavier Education Network (DEN), and is a former chair of the Committee on Teaching Adults for the National Conference on Keyboard Pedagogy, where she serves on the Committee on Research. Dr. Pike has served as president of the Louisiana Music Teachers Association and of the Baton Rouge Music Teachers Association. She has won the Louisiana Music Teachers Association Outstanding Teacher Award, the LSU Tiger Athletic Foundation Undergraduate Teaching Award, and the Arkansas State Music Teachers Association Teacher of the Year Award.

Dr. Pike has presented research papers at international conferences throughout Asia, Eastern and Western Europe, Scandinavia, and North and South America. In the United States, she is regularly invited to present papers and workshops at the Music Teachers National Association, the College Music Society, the Association for Technology in Music Instruction, and the National Conference on Keyboard Pedagogy. Dr. Pike's research interests include distance learning, teaching older adults (third-age students), group teaching techniques, and cognition and human learning. ♩

Table of Contents

Introduction

Guides

Supplementary Material

HOW TO PLAY PIANO

Many people express a desire to learn to play the piano during adulthood; others had some musical training as children but remember little, having not touched an instrument in decades, and wish to relearn lost skills. Although it can be intimidating to learn to play an instrument, if you are guided step by step through the learning process and spend a little time each day refining your technique and acquiring new skills and concepts, you can learn how to play piano.

This course provides a systematic approach to learning core musical concepts that are necessary to play the piano. You will begin by learning about features of the piano keyboard and the importance of fingering by exploring a familiar melody (Beethoven's "Ode to Joy"). You will be encouraged to find a relaxed sitting and playing position at the keyboard and to watch, listen to, and play along with your instructor. As you learn basics about pitch and rhythm, you will read from a modified off-staff notation so you can focus on your fingers and the sound that you are creating as you play. Gradually, you will learn to read traditional notation on the grand staff and learn about and play increasingly complex music. You are encouraged to play along with the instructor as you are learning new skills and concepts and once you have prepared assigned pieces of music.

Core musical concepts and piano skills are introduced and reinforced through music theory, technique exercises, and musical examples. The music is a combination of folk tunes from across the globe, original pieces composed for this course, classical standards from each of the major time periods, and arrangements of music by master composers. You will explore new concepts and be encouraged to make meaningful connections between previously learned and new skills through improvising your own melodies, creating accompaniments to harmonize melodies provided for you, transposing music, and learning incrementally challenging repertoire.

Learning to listen to and evaluate your playing is a key component of this course. There are more than 100 musical examples and exercises that you will play throughout this course. In each piece, you will be guided toward identifying technical and musical issues and provided with useful practice tips and strategies that can enhance your ability to practice effectively and efficiently.

The music that you will learn in the video is available in this accompanying music book. Also included at the end of some video lessons are relevant accompaniment tracks with which you can play along to help you maintain a steady pulse and to complement your performance.

Upon successful completion of this course, you will have played different styles of music; have a basic understanding of piano technique, development of the instrument, music theory, and music history; and have received guidance about refining your goals for future piano study. ♩

LESSON 1

Basic Piano Rhythm and Fingering

In this lesson, you will be introduced to the concept of finger numbers, which help you identify where your fingers should be on the piano at any given moment and can accelerate your learning by helping you play melodies before you know all of the notes on the keyboard or in the musical score. You will also learn how to sit properly at the piano, and you will dive into the fire with some easy improvisation on the black keys. Then, you will gain insight into how different notes are played and discover the important role of rhythm. Finally, you will put it all together and play a portion of Beethoven's "Ode to Joy."

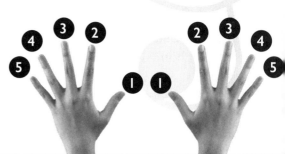

©Suradech14/iStock/Thinkstock

KEY TERMS

DOTTED NOTE: A note head with a dot placed after it that adds half of the value of the regular note.

HALF NOTE: Rhythmic symbol that has an open head and a stem; held for two counts, or beats.

LH: Left hand.

NOTE HEAD: The round part of a rhythmic symbol that provides important information about its note name or pitch, which corresponds with a specific piano key.

PITCH: The specific note that is played on the piano.

QUARTER NOTE: Rhythmic symbol that has a solid black head and a stem; held for one count, or beat.

> Consult the diagram in the Glossary to help you identify musical terms and notation [p. 152].

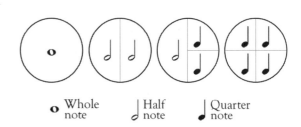

o Whole note | Half note | Quarter note

REST: Silence in music.

RH: Right hand.

RHYTHM: How music is organized in time.

WHOLE NOTE: Rhythmic symbol that has an open head with no stem; held for four counts, or beats.

RESTS

| WHOLE | HALF | QUARTER | EIGHTH |

There is evidence to suggest that music and dance have been part of human expression since practically the beginning of our existence. Thousands of years ago, people used drums and other percussive instruments to accompany dance with rhythm. In fact, we were making music long before we wrote it down or notated it.

But without a written record, a piece of great music was nearly impossible to duplicate. So, notation is our best effort at writing down what we play so that others can reproduce the music later.

Over many hundreds of years, musical notation became codified, but it's essentially a symbolic system. By using dots, lines, and symbols, notation conveys sounds that, to the uninitiated, may not make sense with what we see on the page. But with a little study, we can decode rhythmic symbols.

PRACTICE ASSIGNMENT

- ❏ Wiggle each of your fingers, tap your fingers to your thumb, and say the finger number.

- ❏ Improvise on the black keys. (Try playing with the accompaniment track at the end of the video lesson.)

- ❏ Memorize the value of the quarter, half, dotted half, and whole notes and rests.

- ❏ Play the black-key "Warm-Up" [p. 4]. (Remember your relaxed piano position.)

- ❏ Learn "Ode to Joy" [p. 4] and be able to play along with the instructor.

 PRACTICE TIP

Practicing improvisation can be rewarding, and it can help you integrate new concepts in ways that are personally meaningful. Even if the notes don't quite come out the way you expect as you start improvising, don't worry. It tends to get easier over time.

When improvising in this lesson, listen to the accompaniment and play some notes on your piano. When you find a melody that you like, try to remember the pattern that you just played so you can do it again in the future.

Warm-Up

LH

3 ^{2} $3-$ 3 ^{2} $3-$ 3 ^{2} $3-$

RH

2 ^{3} ^{4} 3 $2---$ 2 ^{3} ^{4} 3 $2---$

Ode to Joy

RH 2 2 ^{3} ^{4} ^{4} 3 2 **RH** 2 2

LH 2 3 3 2 **LH** 2 $2-$

RH 2 2 ^{3} ^{4} ^{4} 3 2 **RH** 2

LH 2 3 3 2 **LH** 2 3 $3-$

LESSON 2

Pitch and Off-Staff Notation

This lesson begins with a review of finger numbers as well as "Ode to Joy." Then, you will learn about meter and time signatures, which appear at the beginning of notated music and help you know how many beats will be in each measure. Next, you will delve into learning about pitch more deeply. Specifically, you will learn to locate C all over the piano keyboard, discover the pitches for the C major 5-finger pattern (the first five notes of the C scale), and learn some new music: "Étude in C Major."

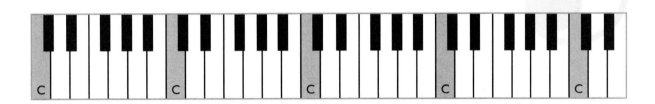

KEY TERMS

BAR LINE: The vertical line that divides the notes into equal numbers of beats.

ÉTUDE: From the French word that means "study," a piece of music focused on a specific skill that is developed with practice.

MAJOR: Describes the type of mode being played in; one of the two most commonly encountered modes in Western classical music; sounds lighter than the minor mode.

MEASURE: The space between each bar line.

METER: The property of music that is based on an underlying, repeating beat rhythm.

SCALE: A group of notes that often move in a stepwise motion.

SHADOWING: A practice step that involves placing your hand over the keys that you will use in a piece and then tapping the keys, without depressing them, and saying the note names.

STAFF: The lines and spaces on which notes and pitches are notated. A staff has five lines and four spaces, and each of these is numbered from bottom to top.

TIME SIGNATURE: The numerical representation at the beginning of a piece used to identify and describe the meter of the piece.

PRACTICE ASSIGNMENT

❑ Clap the four rhythm patterns in this lesson [p. 7].

❑ Play "C Exercise" [p. 8] with the accompaniment track.

❑ Practice the C major 5-finger pattern [p. 8] (separate hands; try hands together for more of a challenge).

❑ Practice "Étude in C Major" [p. 8] and be able to play with the instructor in the video lesson.

❑ Review "Ode to Joy" from lesson 1 [p. 4] (try playing with the accompaniment track) and learn the right hand–only version of "Ode to Joy" [p. 9].

The content of the practice assignments given in this course reflects a very effective way to learn to play the piano. The assignments are crafted so that during the days between your lessons, you'll be working on some new techniques or music. These new skills will be applied in the following lesson, so you'll want to be sure that you've given yourself enough time to assimilate these new concepts. But you will also be reviewing and perfecting repertoire or material from previous lessons. In general, it will take more than one lesson to perfect music and technique, so by staggering the old and the new, you'll always be learning something new, improving your reading and technical skills, and working at the later stages of refining repertoire.

If you are a true beginner, you will not likely achieve perfection the first time or the first day that you practice. But, with a little daily rehearsal, you will improve, slowly but surely. Throughout the course, you will be provided with specific things to listen for and techniques that you can try during your practice. These are all ideas that you should try and that you can add to a metaphorical toolbox of practice strategies.

PRACTICE TIP

When you first look at a musical score, take a quick scan to look at the time signature and starting pitch and subsequent pitch and rhythm patterns. Follow this three-step procedure:

1   *Before playing the pitches, you should understand the rhythmic patterns; you can do this by clapping the rhythm while saying or singing the note names.*

2   *Place your hand over the keys that you will use in the piece and then tap the keys, without depressing them, and say the note names again. This is called shadowing, and it's a great intermediary step between clapping the rhythm and actually playing the notes.*

3   *Play and say the note names.*

Rhythm Patterns

C Exercise

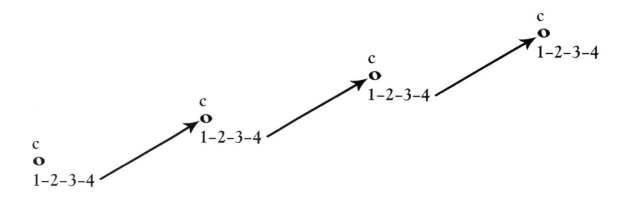

C Major 5-Finger Pattern

All major 5-finger patterns appear on page 164.

Étude in C Major

RH 1   2   3   4   5   5

3/4

C   C   D   D   E   F   G   G   F   E   F   E   D   C

LH 5   4   3   2   1

C   C   D   D   E   F   G   G   F   E   F   E   D   C

Ode to Joy

(right hand only)

LESSON 3

Tonic and Dominant Harmony

In this lesson, you will review the C major 5-finger pattern and practice it with hands together. Next, you will review "Étude in C Major." You will learn about dynamics in music and practice playing forte (loud) and piano (soft); then, you will add these dynamics to "Étude in C Major." You will also learn about tonic and dominant harmony, which you will add to "Ode to Joy," and you will improvise a melody over harmony notes. Finally, you will learn, measure by measure, the melody for a new piece of music by Louis Köhler called the Melodic Tune.

KEY TERMS

DOMINANT: The fifth scale degree.

DYNAMICS: In music, changes in the intensity of the sound.

FORTE: The Italian term for "loud" or "strong," notated as $\boldsymbol{f}$.

HARMONY: Pitches that are played simultaneously, such as chords.

MELODY: The tune of a piece or single pitches, played one after another.

PIANO: The Italian word for "soft," notated as $\boldsymbol{p}$.

REPEAT SIGN: A symbol placed on the score to indicate a repeat (:‖).

TONIC: The first note of the scale being played. Because each note is called a scale degree, most often the tonic is the first scale degree.

Louis Köhler was a German composer and piano teacher who was born in 1820 and died in 1886.

Public domain/Flickr/Public Domain

PRACTICE ASSIGNMENT

❑ Practice the C major 5-finger pattern [p. 8], hands together, with the repeat. You should be able to play it with the instructor on the video or with the accompaniment track, and you should play it at a forte dynamic level and at a piano dynamic level.

❑ Work out a 16-bar improvisation over tonic and dominant left hand notes (remember that there is an accompaniment track that you can play along with).

❑ Practice "Étude in C Major" [p. 12]. Pay close attention to dynamics.

❑ Play "Ode to Joy" with both hands [p. 12] (you'll play the melody entirely with the right hand now, while the left hand plays tonic and dominant notes).

❑ Learn the right hand of Köhler's Melodic Tune [p. 13] and be able to play it before lesson 4.

PRACTICE TIP

If you make a mistake during a lesson or when you are playing with the accompaniment tracks, don't try to go back and correct it; instead, try to look ahead and jump back in—though this takes practice, too! Just be patient and remember that playing and reading music, hands together, is more challenging than it looks and sounds.

Feel free to review this lesson as necessary and practice playing along with the instructor or with the accompaniments that are included in your course materials so that you'll be prepared to play at the correct speed before the next lesson. Take at least a few days to reinforce these new concepts and the new music before moving on to lesson 4. In fact, many people need several days or a week before they are ready for lesson 4.

Étude in C Major

(with dynamic markings)

RH 1   2   3   4   5 [5]

C   C   D   D   E   F   G   G   F   E   F   E   D   C

f

[9]

LH 5   4   3   2   1 [13]

C   C   D   D   E   F   G   G   F   E   F   E   D   C

p   *f*

Ode to Joy

(both hands)

RH

E E F G | G F E D | C C D E | E D D

LH

C | G | C | G

    I   V   I   V

E E F G | G F E D | C C D E | D C C

C | G | C | G   C

    I   V   I   V   I

Melodic Tune

(right hand only)

Köhler
arr. Pike

RH 3 1 3 5   3   [5] 4   3
3/4 E E E C E G   E   F F F F E   E

[9] 3   [13] 5 4 2   1
    E E E C E G   E   G F D G F D C   C

(both hands)

RH 3 1 3 5   3   [5] 4   3
3/4 E E C E G   E   F   F F   F E   E

LH 3/4 C   C   C   C   G   G   C   C

5   1   5
I   V   I

[9] 3   [13] 5 4 2   1
p   E E E C E G   E   f G F D G F D C   C

    C   C   C   C   G   G   C   C

5   1   5
I   V   I

LESSON 4

Intervals and Basic Notation

This lesson begins with an explanation of tempo that will be applied to the C major 5-finger pattern. Then, you will explore new 5-finger patterns for G major and D major. Next, you will learn about the interval of a 2nd (called a step), which is one note, or pitch, name to the very next pitch name, or the movement from a line note to a space note on a staff; as well as learn about the interval of a 3rd (called a skip), which on a staff is the movement from a line note to a line note or from a space note to a space note. Then, you will play the C major 5-finger pattern at a forte dynamic as well as play "Ode to Joy" with dynamics, playing one hand forte and the other hand piano. You will also try to play Köhler's Melodic Tune at a goal tempo with hands together. Finally, you will learn four landmark notes and try to connect what you know about the "Ode to Joy" and Melodic Tune pitches to those notes on the staff.

KEY TERMS

BASS: Lower notes or sounds; notated on a bass staff and indicated with a bass clef (𝄢).

INTERVAL: The distance between two notes.

INTERVALLIC READING: Reading by referencing specific landmark notes and then using the intervals to figure out the subsequent notes.

LANDMARK NOTES: Notes whose location on the keyboard are learned well that help the player figure out other notes' locations.

INTERVALS OF A STEP

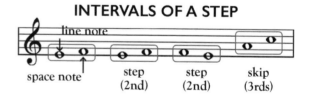

LANDMARK NOTES

METRONOME: A simple device that you can program to click at a particular tempo, measured in beats per minute (bpm).

TEMPO: How fast or slow music is being played.

TRANSPOSE: To transfer a melody into another key so that it begins on a different note or pitch.

TREBLE: Higher notes or sounds; notated on a treble staff and indicated with a treble clef ( ).

PRACTICE ASSIGNMENT

❑ Get a metronome or download a metronome app.

❑ Practice the C, D, and G major 5-finger patterns (goal tempo: quarter note = 132).

❑ Memorize your landmark notes and start trying to identify other pitches around these notes.

❑ Play Köhler's Melodic Tune with both hands and try reading the notation [p. 16] (goal tempo: quarter note = 80).

❑ Play "Ode to Joy" [p. 17].

❑ Shake out your arms and take short breaks during your practice.

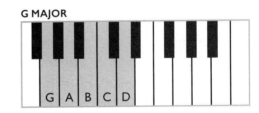

 PRACTICE TIP

When we want to be very specific about the tempo of a piece, we give a metronome marking. In many of your practice assignments from here on, you will be provided with a goal tempo that includes a metronome marking.

If the tempo is noted as a quarter note = 80, turn your metronome to 80 beats per minute, let it click about eight times so you really internalize the tempo, and then begin to play—one note with each click of the metronome.

Melodic Tune

(both hands)

Ode to Joy

(both hands)

Y ou will likely have to work on balancing the melody and harmony in "Ode to Joy." Most people find it very difficult to play one hand louder than the other initially, but hopefully you will improve each time you practice.

LESSON 5

Major Chords and Simple Accompaniment

This lesson will begin by playing Köhler's Melodic Tune straight through at the goal tempo and then with some extra accompaniment notes; you will also try to balance the melody (by keeping it louder) and the harmony (by keeping it softer). Then, you will review the G and D major 5-finger patterns as well as learn the 5-finger patterns for E and A major; after this lesson, you will know C, D, E, G, and A major 5-finger patterns and chords. You will also learn about another interval: a 5th, which on a staff is the movement from a line to a line with one line in between or from a space to a space with one space in between. Finally, you will work through a version of "When the Saints Go Marching In," which you will learn by reading the musical notation on the grand staff.

KEY TERMS

BLOCKED: Form of playing chords in which all notes are played at once.

BROKEN: Form of playing chords in which the pianist plays the bottom note, middle note, top note, and then back down.

CHORD: Three or more notes played together; often used to create harmony.

LEGER LINE: A snippet of a line that is added above or below a musical staff to lengthen its range.

SLUR: A curved line that connects notes of different pitches that should be played smoothly (legato).

TIE: A curved line that connects notes of the same pitch across a bar line.

TRIAD: A three-note chord consisting of a root note and 3rd and 5th intervals.

❏ Practice 5-finger scales and chords in C, D, E, G, and A major (goal tempo: quarter note = 132; this is the speed of the accompaniment tracks).

❏ Memorize the space notes for treble and bass clef (FACE and ACEG).

❏ Practice Köhler's Melodic Tune [p. 16], hands together, with dynamics and balance the melody and harmony parts.

❏ Practice "When the Saints Go Marching In" [p. 20] (goal tempo: quarter note = 132).

❏ Review anything from previous lessons that you would like to learn more securely or just play for fun.

E MAJOR

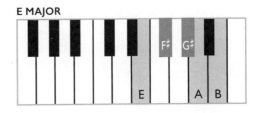

A MAJOR

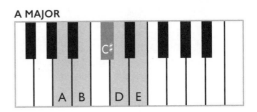

 PRACTICE TIP

When playing along with the instructor, try to stay on track and keep playing even if you make a few mistakes. If you make mistakes, isolate the problem spots and practice them until you can play them with ease, before integrating them back into the entire piece. You might make a note of these places on your score so that you can go back to them during your practice after the lesson.

When the Saints Go Marching In

Traditional
arr. Pike

Once you have gotten comfortable with the pieces from this lesson, play along with the instructor on the video. This will help you get a sense of where you have succeeded and spots that might still need some review.

LESSON 6

Fourths, Accidentals, and Relaxation

This lesson will begin with a warm-up for your fingers by playing the 5-finger patterns and their related chords. Then, you will learn two more major 5-finger patterns, F and B, which means that you will know all of the major 5-finger scales that begin on a white key. Next, you will learn about accidentals—sharp, flat, natural—and examine measures of music that contain accidentals and decide which notes are sharp, flat, or natural. You will also play "When the Saints Go Marching In," focusing on exaggerating the dynamics. Then, you will be introduced to the interval of a 4th, which on a staff goes from a line to a space or from a space to a line with two notes in between; you will learn to identify the interval of a 4th as well as learn a short new piece called "Aura Lee" that features the interval of a 4th. You will also be introduced to the melody of a piece called "Woodland Jaunt." Finally, this lesson will address healthy playing and staying relaxed at the piano.

KEY TERMS

ACCIDENTAL: A sign—such as a sharp, flat, or natural sign—that is placed in front of a note on the staff to indicate a change in pitch.

ENHARMONIC: Relating to notes that sound like the same pitch and look like the same key on the piano but are written differently on the staff.

FLAT (♭): The symbol used in music to indicate that a note or pitch should be lowered by a half step; when a flat is placed in front of a note, that note remains flat for the entire measure, unless otherwise indicated.

HARMONIC INTERVAL: A type of interval in which the notes are played simultaneously.

MELODIC INTERVAL: A type of interval in which the notes are played in sequence, one after the other.

NATURAL SIGN (♮): A sign indicating that a note should return to its normal, or natural, pitch; just like the other accidentals (flat and sharp), the natural sign is placed before the pitch and on the same line or in the same space as the note being altered and lasts for the remainder of the measure.

SHARP (♯): The symbol used in music to indicate that a note or pitch should be raised by a half step; when a sharp is placed in front of a note, that note remains sharp for the entire measure, unless otherwise indicated.

PRACTICE ASSIGNMENT

- ❑ Do a 3- to 5-minute physical warm-up before going to the piano or keyboard.

- ❑ Warm up your fingers with these 5-finger patterns and chords: C, D, E, F, G, A, and B major.

- ❑ Learn "Aura Lee" [p. 24] with both hands (goal tempo: quarter note = 108; play with accompaniment).

- ❑ Practice "Woodland Jaunt" [p. 24]. Play the melody with the accompaniment and try it slowly with hands together (accompaniment tempo: quarter note = 132).

- ❑ Review an older repertoire piece.

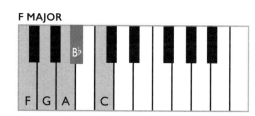

F MAJOR

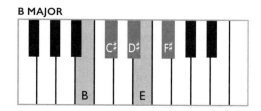

B MAJOR

🎼 PRACTICE TIPS

- ↝ *When you warm up, you should play through all seven of the major key scales and chords that you know. Not only will this help you become familiar with the scales and chords, but it will also help to develop finger facility, which will be required in more advanced pieces.*

- ↝ *Take short breaks throughout each practice session.*

- ↝ *End your practice by doing a light stretch of your arms and shoulders and a physical cooldown.*

HEALTHY PLAYING AND STAYING RELAXED

When playing the piano, it is important to maintain a relaxed hand and body position. The following are steps that you can take before, during, and after practice to stay healthy and prevent injury.

- You should never feel pain when you play. If something hurts, stop right away and try to figure out where the tension is coming from so that you can prevent it the next time you sit at the piano.

- Maintain good piano position. Don't allow your head to jut forward, which can cause you to get out of alignment and lead to neck, shoulder, and back tension.

- Maintain good hand and finger position. You can always put your hands down by your sides or over your knees to remember what the healthy hand position looks and feels like. Once you play a key on the piano, relax your hand; there is no need to maintain pressure when holding a note.

- Warm up the larger muscles and the body before and after practice and take short breaks to avoid sitting in one position for an extended period of time. Pay attention to your body and you'll discover when you should take breaks; in the beginning, it's a good idea to stand up and take a quick break or stretch every 15 or 20 minutes.

Try to do some physical warm-ups before you sit down to do your finger warm-ups at the piano. Then, take breaks and do stretches during practice and after you finish practicing; physical cooldowns help keep the muscles limber.

During physical warm-ups and cooldowns:

- Breathe deeply, from the diaphragm (during this time, be aware of any tension and try to gently release it).

- Walk around the room or march in place for 3 to 5 minutes to get the blood flowing. You can use this time to think about what you're going to work on during practice and plan your practice session.

- Swing your arms.

During practice/breaks:

- Do shoulder shrugs and rolls.

- Do the backstroke.

Wringing an imaginary towel, shaking out the arms, and a gentle hand massage can prevent injury and soreness from pronation, which is the way you hold your arms at the piano for extended periods of time when you play and practice.

Aura Lee

Poulton
arr. Pike

Woodland Jaunt

LESSON 7

Primary Chords

This lesson will delve more deeply into chords. You will even harmonize melodies with three-note chords, rather than with just single notes or two-note harmonic intervals. The lesson begins with a finger warm-up that includes all seven of the 5-finger patterns and chords, beginning on G and working around to F. Then, you will learn about primary chord progressions, practice progressions in F and C major, and improvise a possible melody. You will also play "Aura Lee" and "Woodland Jaunt" from the previous lesson to check on your progress. Finally, you will learn the first four measures of a piece by Köhler called Melody in G.

KEY TERMS

CADENCE: A chord sequence that resolves at the end of a piece or phrase and that should sound and feel like a resting place.

CHORD TONES: The notes contained in each chord.

DOMINANT CHORD: The chord that is built on the fifth scale degree.

NONCHORD TONES: Notes that are not chord tones.

PRIMARY CHORD PROGRESSION: A tonic-subdominant-dominant-tonic progression that is the most basic chord progression at the heart of Western music.

PRIMARY CHORDS: The three most commonly used chords in any key; the tonic (first scale degree), subdominant (fourth scale degree), and dominant (fifth scale degree) tones of the scale.

RESOLUTION: The quality that certain chords have when they lead toward or have a tendency to go toward certain other chords, resulting in a very satisfying sound.

SUBDOMINANT CHORD: The chord that is built on the fourth scale degree.

TONIC CHORD: The chord that is built on the first scale degree.

PRACTICE ASSIGNMENT

☐ Remember to do physical warm-ups, cooldowns, and stretches.

☐ Practice these 5-finger patterns and chords: C, D, E, F, G, A, and B major. Start on a different key each day, and play increasingly faster (goal tempo: quarter note = 120).

☐ Review "When the Saints Go Marching In" [p. 20].

☐ Practice the primary chord progressions in C and F major [p. 27].

☐ Practice "Woodland Jaunt" with primary chords [p. 28] (goal tempo: quarter note = 176).

☐ Practice Köhler's Melody in G, op. 218, no. 18 [p. 28] (tempo: quarter note = 100).

☐ Improvise in F major and notate your improvisation on the staff below. (More blank staff pages are available in the back of this book.)

 PRACTICE TIP

It's recommended that you begin your 5-finger warm-up in a different key every few days—partially because you don't want to get in a rut, but mainly because of human attention and its role in learning new things. Humans tend to focus really well at the beginning of an exercise (or even a lesson), so the first few scales get better. However, if your concentration and attention wane toward the middle or end of your routine, the musical result is that the last few keys don't progress or improve as much as the first keys. The result after several days of practice is that the first keys keep improving while the last keys don't ever get quite as comfortable.

Primary Chord Progressions

C MAJOR

I   IV   V

I   IV   V

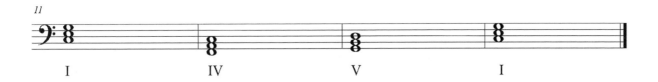

I   IV   V   I

F MAJOR

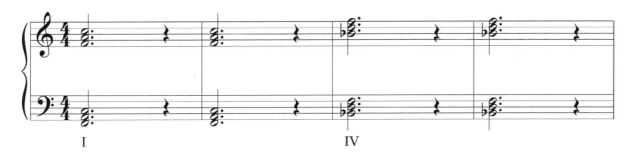

I   IV

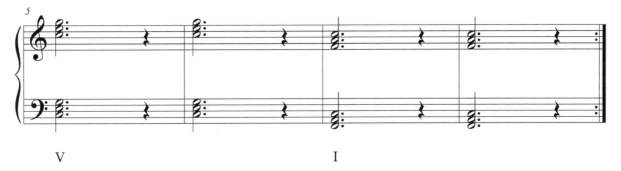

V   I

All major primary chord progressions appear on page 164.

Woodland Jaunt

(with primary chords)

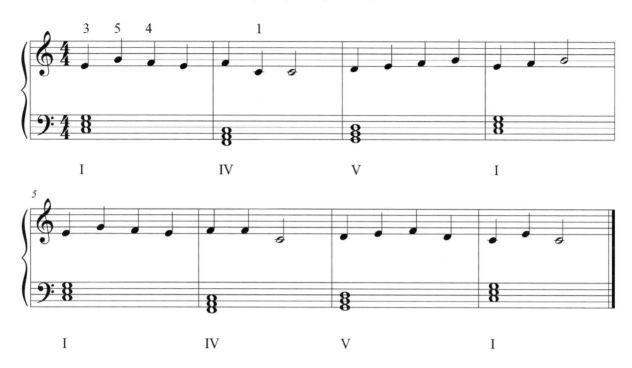

Melody in G, op. 218, no. 18

Köhler
arr. Pike

LESSON 8

Transposition at the Piano

This lesson begins with a warm-up of 5-finger patterns, chords, and chord progressions, starting with F major. Then, you will run through your improvisation in F. Next, you will review the key of C major and play a piece in that key: "Woodland Jaunt." Then, you will harmonize the "Woodland Jaunt" melody using chords from the C major primary chord progression, and you will transpose this piece into the key of F. You will also transpose "Ode to Joy" into the key of F (after playing it in the key of C, as you learned it). In addition, you will review "When the Saints Go Marching In" in the key of C, as you've been practicing it, and then transpose it into the key of G major. Then, you will learn a new combination of primary chords that you will turn into a blues piece in the next lesson. Finally, you will play Köhler's Melody in G all the way through.

PRACTICE ASSIGNMENT

❑ Practice the 5-finger patterns and chords (quarter note = 140).

❑ Practice left hand chord progression in C, D, F, and G major.

❑ Play "Ode to Joy" [p. 17] (C and F major).

❑ Play "When the Saints Go Marching In" [p. 20] (C and G major).

❑ Play "Woodland Jaunt" [p. 28] (C and F major).

❑ Play Köhler's Melody [p. 28] (G and D major).

❑ Practice the left hand 12-bar G progression [p. 31].

PRACTICE TIPS

❧ Warm up in the key of the piece that you will be practicing so that you can familiarize yourself with the notes of the scale. Within the piece, you can expect those notes, and it trains your fingers about where they will need to be. It's a good idea to review the chords that you will likely encounter in the harmony, too.

❧ The easiest way to think about transposing "Woodland Jaunt" from the key of C to F major is to move your hands into the F major 5-finger pattern and instead of reading the actual note names, read the intervals (see below).

Woodland Jaunt

(transposition steps)

12-Bar G Progression

(left hand only)

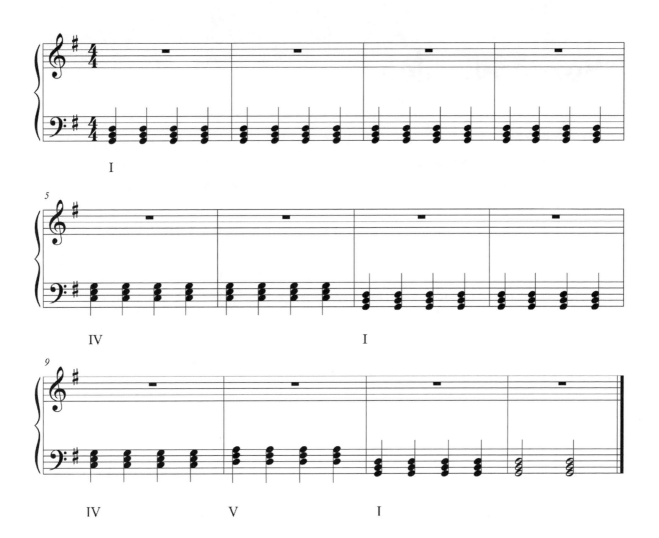

LESSON 9

Chord Inversions

Although you won't learn a lot of new music in this lesson, you will begin to set the technical foundation on which so much piano music is based. This lesson will make your musical life richer by building on the way you play chords and harmonies. The lesson begins by reviewing several of the pieces that you've been working on since the previous lesson so that you can assess your progress. Then, you will learn the key signatures for four keys. Next, you will play the 12-bar progression that you learned in the previous lesson, and you will be introduced to the blues scale. You will also learn some alternate ways to play chords—ways that will ultimately be easier and sound better in chord progressions. Finally, you will learn four triads and inversions as well as the most basic arpeggio.

KEY TERMS

12-BAR BLUES: A chord progression that has three four-bar phrases and is one of the typical blues progressions.

ARPEGGIO: A broken chord.

FIGURED BASS: A bass line that has the harmonies shown by numbers, or figures, rather than written out as chords.

INVERSIONS: The different positions that chords can be put in when altering the way the notes on the staff are stacked up for each chord.

KEY SIGNATURE: Indicates the sharps or flats in any given key and is found at the beginning of the staff, immediately following the treble or bass clef; the order of the sharps and flats in the key signature is always the same.

ROOT: The chord's name or which scale degree it's built upon.

ROOT POSITION: When the name of the chord, or root, is the bottom note.

In earlier periods of music, the keyboard part in chamber music was not written out completely; rather, the right-hand melody and the figured bass would be written in. The keyboardist would play or improvise the keyboard part during performance based on the figured bass. Musicians call this skill "realizing" the bass line. It is a skill that is rarely taught in beginning piano lessons in the 21st century. As a result, when pianists get to college, many find it difficult to realize figured bass on the spot.

PRACTICE ASSIGNMENT

- ❏ Memorize the key signatures for C, G, D, and F major.

- ❏ Play Köhler's Melody [p. 28] transposed to D major.

- ❏ Practice the C major arpeggio [p. 34].

- ❏ Practice C, G, D, and A major triads and inversions (separate hands) with correct fingering (quarter note = 0) [p. 34].

- ❏ Practice the blues scale in G [p. 36].

- ❏ Play the 12-bar blues [p. 36] (work on the right hand; try with the left hand a few times).

- ❏ Review any other repertoire from previous lessons.

- ❏ Transpose previously learned repertoire into new keys for an added challenge!

KEY SIGNATURES

C MAJOR

D MAJOR

F MAJOR

G MAJOR

C Major Arpeggio

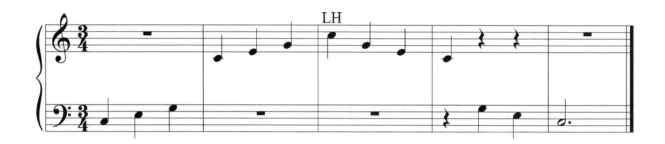

Triads and Inversions

The note following the slash is the lowest pitch in the chord.

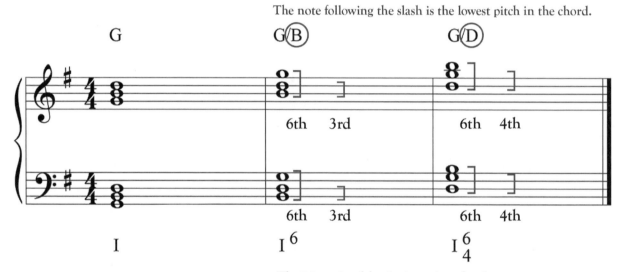

The 3 is omitted for 1st inversion chords.

C MAJOR

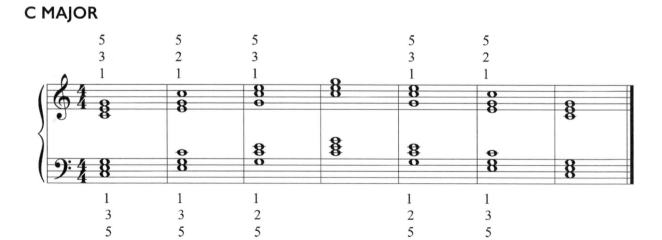

D MAJOR

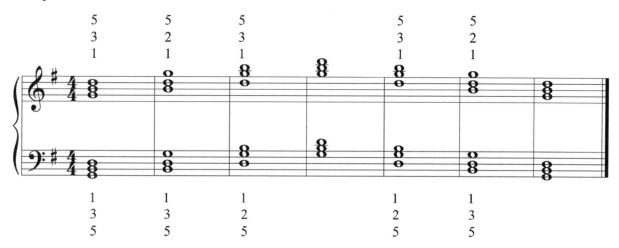

G MAJOR

A MAJOR

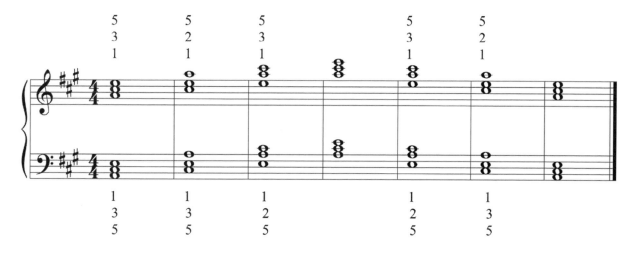

Blues Scale in G

12-Bar Blues

LESSON 10

Chord Progressions and Arpeggios

In this lesson, you will explore the dominant chord more closely and tie the inversions from the previous lesson and this lesson into a new, and practical, chord progression, which you will transpose to various keys. You will begin by playing triads and inversions in several keys. Then, you will learn "Arpeggio Étude" to reinforce the C major arpeggio. Next, while taking a closer look at the dominant chord, you will discover what a four-note chord looks like. You will also become familiar with two cadences: the dominant 7th to tonic and the subdominant to tonic. The lesson will end by introducing you to a piece called "Summer Sunrise."

PRACTICE ASSIGNMENT

❏ Practice the I-IV$^6_4$-I cadence and the I-V$^6_5$-I cadence in C major as shown below.

SUBDOMINANT TO TONIC

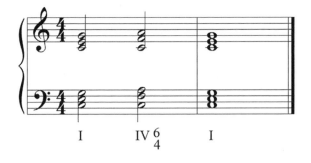

DOMINANT 7TH TO TONIC

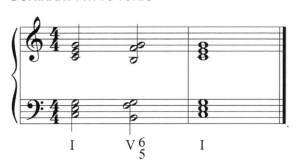

- ❑ Practice the I-IV$^6_4$-I-V$^6_5$-I primary chord progression in C major as shown below (goal tempo: quarter note = 80).

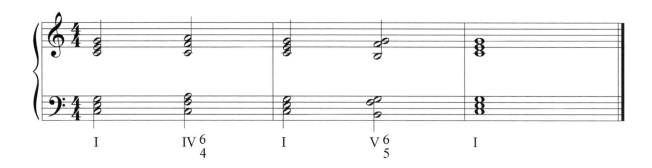

- ❑ Play triads and inversions in C, D, E, F, G, A, and B major. (C, D, G, and A are shown in the previous lesson.)

- ❑ Play "Arpeggio Étude" [p. 40].

- ❑ Play "Summer Sunrise" [p. 40] using practice steps (goal tempo: quarter note = 112).

- ❑ Improvise a melody over your left hand chord progression in C major and notate it below.

- ❑ Remember physical warm-ups, cooldowns, and breathing.

- ❑ Review any older repertoire that could be improved.

 PRACTICE TIP

When playing triads and inversions with hands together, don't try to move both hands at once until you are completely comfortable. Rather, move the right hand first and then the left—just move them quickly so you can play the next inversion on time. You'll actually "spot place" your hands over the keys before you depress them. This will give you a chance to make minor adjustments to finger placement before you play a wrong note.

Improvisation in C

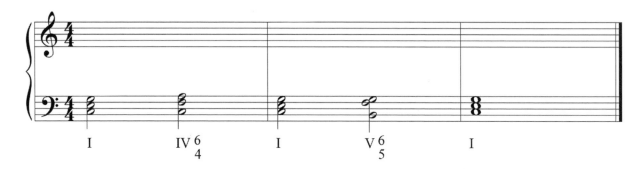

Triads and Inversions

E MAJOR

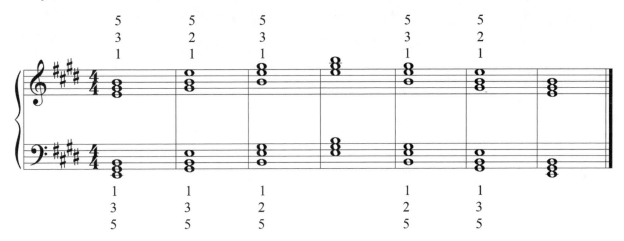

F MAJOR

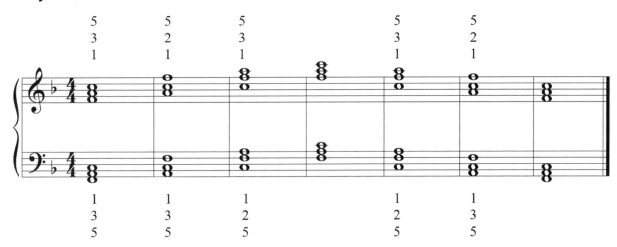

B MAJOR

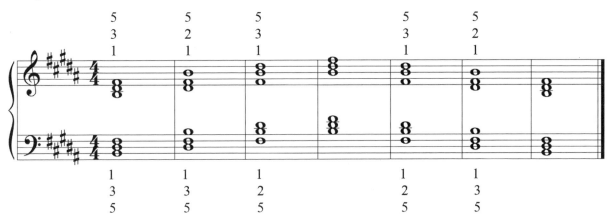

Arpeggio Étude

Summer Sunrise

LESSON 11

Accompaniment Patterns and Sight-Reading

This lesson will begin by reviewing "Arpeggio Étude" as well as the new version of the primary chord progression in C. Then, you will review your transposition skills by figuring out the melody for "Summer Sunrise" in G major. You will also learn a new étude, called "Chord Étude 1," that will help you learn the primary chord progression with inversions in another key. Next, you will learn three accompaniment patterns: the broken chord pattern, the waltz-style pattern, and the Alberti bass. You will also learn an arrangement of a composition by Carl Czerny, who studied piano with Beethoven, called the Waltz in G. Finally, you will be introduced to three new major 5-finger patterns, each of which has a black key as the tonic note.

KEY TERMS

BLOCKING: A practice technique that can be applied to any piece that contains chord patterns and involves playing each complete chord on the downbeat.

MEZZO FORTE: The Italian term for "moderately loud," notated as **mf**.

SEQUENCE: Repeating patterns starting on different pitches.

SIGHT-READING: The practice of trying to play a piece of music as well as you can on the first try.

 PRACTICE TIP

During your practice, when you think you have the dynamics of a piece down, consider recording yourself on your phone and then listening to it. Your dynamics may not be as pronounced as you think they are; as a performer you have to learn to exaggerate your dynamic contrasts.

PRACTICE ASSIGNMENT

- ❏ Review the 5-finger patterns and chords, including the new patterns: D♭, E♭, and A♭ major.

- ❏ Practice primary chord progressions, with inversions, in C, G, D, and F major [lessons 9 and 10].

- ❏ Play "Summer Sunrise" in C major [p. 40] and transpose into G major.

- ❏ Practice sight-reading [p. 43].

- ❏ Practice the three accompaniment patterns with left hand in C, G, and F major [p. 43].

- ❏ Play "Chord Étude" [p. 44].

- ❏ Play Czerny's Waltz in G, op. 777, no. 8 [p. 45].

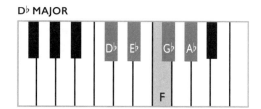

D♭ MAJOR

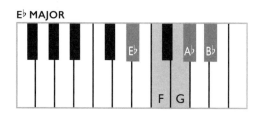

E♭ MAJOR

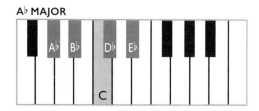

A♭ MAJOR

SIGHT-READING STEPS

Follow these five steps to ensure that you play your best the first time, keeping in mind that the pieces you sight-read should always be easier than the music you are working on:

1 Scan the music to identify familiar rhythm patterns. Tap the rhythm hands together, keeping a steady pulse.

2 Identify your starting pitches and place the correct fingers on those.

3 Shadow the hands separately, noting intervals.

4 Shadow the hands together.

5 Play the piece out loud. Remember to choose an appropriate tempo.

Sight-Reading

Accompaniment Patterns

BROKEN CHORD

WALTZ-STYLE

ALBERTI BASS

Chord Étude

Waltz in G, op. 777, no. 8

Czerny
arr. Pike

LESSON 12

Harmonization and Damper Pedal

In this lesson, you will learn a new key signature, harmonize some melodies with accompaniment patterns, and begin some new techniques that you will need in the next lesson. You will use the practice technique of blocking as well as review one of the primary chord progressions that you practiced. You will learn the key signature for D major, and you will be exposed to two harmonization examples. Next, you will be introduced to the damper pedal, and you will do a pedal exercise. Then, you will learn two technical exercises—a finger-crossover exercise and a hand-lifting exercise—that will allow you to practice hand shifts before you experience melodies that expand a little above or below the notes contained in the 5-finger pattern. Finally, you will learn the Gb major 5-finger pattern.

KEY TERMS

BACKWARD REPEAT SIGN: Indicates that at some point subsequently you'll see a repeat sign, but instead of going all the way back to the beginning of the score, you'll repeat the segment of music from this sign (notated as ‖:).

DAMPER PEDAL: The pedal on the far right of your piano—regardless of how many pedals your piano has—that you depress with your right foot to lift the dampers (which contain the felt that dampens the strings, or stops them from vibrating), causing all of the strings to ring until you release the pedal.

Your ability to listen to and evaluate your playing and to correctly identify problem spots is a critical part of improving your playing during practice. Once you know where the problem is, you can slow it down, isolate the passage, and work out the details.

PRACTICE ASSIGNMENT

❑ Review all 12 of the major 5-finger patterns and chords, including G♭ and B♭ major.

❑ Practice primary chord progressions in C, G, D, and F major.

❑ Practice the two harmonization examples below.

❑ Do "Pedal Exercise 1" [p. 48].

❑ Practice the two technical exercises from this lesson [p. 49].

❑ Review "Chord Étude 1" [p. 44] (you'll play it in the next lesson).

❑ Review Czerny's Waltz [p. 45] and try to polish it.

❑ Review anything from previous lessons that you would like to improve or that you just have fun playing.

> All major 5-finger patterns and primary chord progressions appear on page 164.

G♭ MAJOR

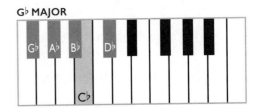

B♭ MAJOR

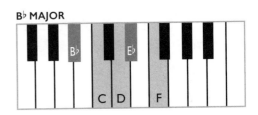

Harmonizations

Harmonize this melody with a **Waltz bass** accompaniment pattern.

D MAJOR   I   IV$^6_4$ I   V$^6_5$ I

Harmonize this melody with an **Alberti bass** accompaniment pattern.

F MAJOR   I   IV$^6_4$ V$^6_5$ I   V$^6_5$ I

THE DAMPER PEDAL

Regardless of whether your piano has two or three pedals, the damper pedal is the one on the far right of your piano, and you will use your right foot to depress it. When you depress this pedal, it lifts the dampers—which contain the felt that dampens the strings, or stops them from vibrating. So, when the damper pedal is depressed, all of the strings will ring until you release the pedal.

If you have a grand piano, you can see the dampers lift up off of the strings when you press the pedal. On an upright piano, the strings are strung vertically, so the dampers move off of the strings in a vertical motion (toward where you are sitting) until you release the pedal, and the dampers move back to rest on the strings.

If you are using a digital piano, the pedal replicates the sound of the dampers releasing from the strings. If you own a keyboard that doesn't have a pedal, check the back of the instrument; most have a quarter-inch jack or port for plugging in a foot pedal. If possible, purchase a universal sustain pedal so you can experience the effect of using the pedal when you play.

Keep your heel on the floor as you depress and lift your foot off the pedal. This serves two purposes:

1   It allows you to have much more control over the pedal. Sometimes you will only depress the pedal partway, or you may need to make quick changes that require more control.

2   Your quadriceps will become very tired if you are constantly lifting your entire foot when you pedal.

Pedal Exercise 1

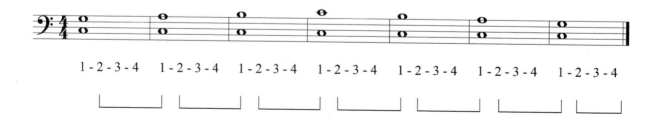

1 - 2 - 3 - 4   1 - 2 - 3 - 4   1 - 2 - 3 - 4   1 - 2 - 3 - 4   1 - 2 - 3 - 4   1 - 2 - 3 - 4   1 - 2 - 3 - 4

Technical Exercises

LIFTS

CROSSOVERS

G MAJOR   D MAJOR   C MAJOR

LESSON 13

Minor Finger Patterns and Chords

In this lesson, you will warm up with some major 5-finger patterns and chords. Then, you will review the two harmonization examples from the previous lesson and then learn a new one, whose melody is the American folk song "Skip to My Lou." You will also be exposed to two new sight-reading examples using the sight-reading steps that were introduced in lesson 11. Then, you will figure out the whole- and half-step pattern for the minor 5-finger scale and play "Minor Étude," which is in D minor. Next, you will learn a new pedal exercise and play "Chord Étude 1" with the pedal, which creates a nice sound by allowing the notes to ring and letting you change chords without any break in the sound. Finally, you will learn a new hand-shifting exercise.

KEY TERMS

LEAD LINE: A melody that is presented with the chord symbols above it instead of having Roman numerals; common in piano and vocal scores, particularly in books that have Broadway tunes.

MINOR: Describes the type of mode being played in; one of the two most commonly encountered modes in Western classical music; sounds darker than the major mode.

MODALITY: Playing in a given mode, such as major or minor.

PRACTICE ASSIGNMENT

- ☐ Play all major 5-finger patterns, broken chords, and blocked chords.

- ☐ Play C, D, E, G, and A minor scales, broken chords, and blocked chords.

 PRACTICE TIP

Because you now know all 12 major 5-finger patterns, it is recommended that you play half of them each time you sit down to practice.

❑ Play the primary chord progressions in C, G, D, and F major.

❑ Do "3-2-1 Hand Shifts" [below].

❑ Review "Pedal Exercise 1" [p. 48] and do "Pedal Exercise 2" [below].

❑ Play "Chord Étude 1" [p. 44] with the pedal.

❑ Practice lead line harmonizations from lesson 12 [p. 47].

❑ Practice sight-reading [p. 52].

❑ Practice "Minor Étude" [p. 53].

❑ Practice "Skip to My Lou" [p. 53].

3-2-1 Hand Shifts

Pedal Exercise 2

Sight-Reading

EXERCISE 1

EXERCISE 2

Minor Étude

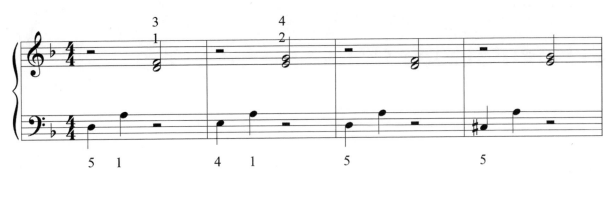

Skip to My Lou

Traditional

LESSON 14

Articulation: Legato and Staccato

This lesson will allow you to explore techniques that will add to the musicality and artistry of your performance, starting with legato and staccato articulation. Then, you will learn two more minor 5-finger patterns: F minor and B minor. Next, you will be introduced to two additional technique warm-ups, the first of which combines staccato and legato articulation and the second of which is another finger-crossover exercise. You will also practice using the pedal, including experimenting with adding it to "Minor Étude" and developing your pedal technique by playing using an overlapping pedal. Then, you will play "Skip To My Lou" with both hands and add a modified waltz bass accompaniment pattern—an oop-pah, oom-pah accompaniment pattern. Next, you will learn the primary chord progression in A and D minor. Finally, you will be introduced to the theme from a piece by Cornelius Gurlitt called "At School" and an arrangement called "Dance" by Diabelli.

The primary chord progression in any minor key is very similar to major primary chord progressions, but there are some important differences. Just as in the major keys, the minor primary chord progression involves playing the tonic, subdominant, and dominant chords; however, in minor keys, the tonic and subdominant chords are minor chords, so they will sound and feel slightly different than what you've become accustomed to playing in the major keys.

KEY TERMS

ARTICULATION: In music, the quality of whether notes are connected to each other or detached.

LEGATO: The Italian term for "tied together," a type of articulation where the notes are connected and played smoothly; notated with a slur (curved line).

NONLEGATO: An articulation that indicates to play the notes somewhat detached from one to the next.

OCTAVE SIGN: A sign placed above the staff to mean play one octave higher (*8va*) or placed below the staff to mean play one octave lower (*8vb*).

STACCATO: The Italian term for "detached" or "disconnected," a type of articulation where the notes are short, or crisp and detached; played even shorter than nonlegato; notated with a dot above or below the notehead (♩̇ ♪).

PRACTICE TIP

Drop your arm and wrist into legato notes and gently lift your arm and wrist on staccato notes.

PRACTICE ASSIGNMENT

❑ Play all major 5-finger patterns (hands together); be sure to practice with legato and staccato articulation.

> All minor 5-finger patterns appear on page 167.

❑ Play the minor 5-finger patterns (hands together) legato and staccato (keys: C, D, E, F, G, A, and B minor).

❑ Play the primary chord progression in A and D minor.

❑ Play "Skip to My Lou" [p. 53] with the left hand oom-pah accompaniment.

❑ Do "Overlapping Pedal Exercise" [p. 56].

❑ Play "Staccato and Legato Warm-Up" [p. 56].

❑ Play "3rd Crossover Warm-Up" [p. 57].

❑ Play the theme from "At School" by Gurlitt [p. 57].

❑ Play "Dance" by Diabelli [p. 58].

When you play legato, you are carefully calibrating when your fingers play. And although your ear is your most valuable tool for recognizing if you are playing legato correctly, if you remember to depress one finger as the next is lifting the key, you should achieve a legato sound.

If there is too much overlap—if you don't lift the finger soon enough—as you are depressing the next finger, the sound will be muddy or blurry. When you hear this, try to adjust by lifting the first finger sooner. However, if there is a gap in the sound as you switch from one finger to the next, simply depress the keys sooner as you go from one note to the next.

Overlapping Pedal Exercise

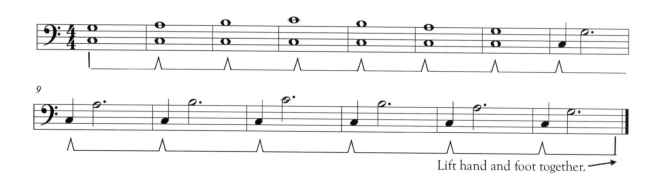

Lift hand and foot together. ⟶

Staccato and Legato Warm-Up

3rd Crossover Warm-Up

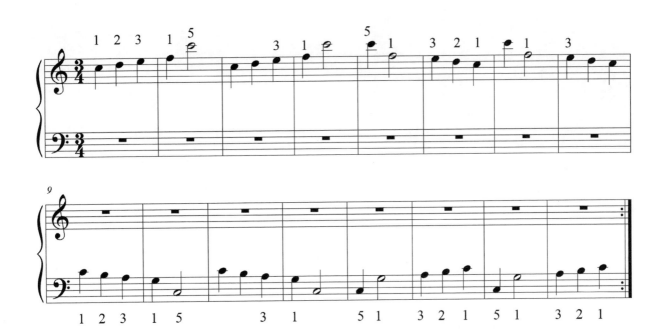

At School, op. 74, no. 4

Gurlitt
arr. Pike

Dance

Diabelli
arr. Pike

LESSON 15

One-Octave Major Scales and Major Intervals

This lesson begins by playing "Dance" by Diabelli, with hands together and maintaining a steady tempo throughout, and then assesses the technical details of the piece. Then, you will review the D minor 5-finger pattern and chord progression and play "Staccato and Legato Warm-Up," transposing the first six measures into D minor. Next, you will dissect and practice a new piece called "Minor Romp." You will also finish learning the remainder of the major scale, including the one-octave C major, G major, and D major scales, called 2-hand tetrachord scales. Then, you will play the first eight measures of "3rd Crossover Warm-Up," transposing it into D major. You will also explore intervals in more detail—specifically the larger 6th, 7th, and octave intervals. Finally, you will be introduced to another new piece, an étude titled "A 'Türk-ish' Tune" that is meant to prepare you for a piece by a composer named Türk.

KEY TERMS

CRESCENDO: To gradually get louder or stronger, abbreviated cres. (or cresc.) or represented as a long less-than sign in mathematics.

DECRESCENDO: See **DIMINUENDO**.

DIMINUENDO: To gradually get softer, abbreviated dim. or represented as a long greater-than sign in mathematics.

RELATIVE MINOR: Major and minor scales that have the same key signature.

TETRACHORD PATTERNS: A series of four notes with a specific pattern of whole steps and half steps.

CRESCENDO

DECRESCENDO

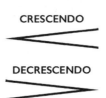

PRACTICE TIP

There is a trick to finding the relative minor key: Once you've identified the major key, put your finger on that note and then go down three half steps (don't count the note that you start on).

PRACTICE ASSIGNMENT

❑ Play the 2-hand tetrachord major scales (1 octave each): C, G, D, A, and F major.

❑ Play the one-octave scale for D, G, and C major with separate hands [p. 61].

❑ Do "Overlapping Pedal Exercise" [p. 56].

❑ Play "Dance" by Diabelli, [p. 58] focusing on musical details and technique.

❑ Play "Minor Romp" [p. 62] with hands together.

❑ Play "A 'Türk-ish' Tune" [p. 62] (get comfortable with separate hands; try hands together slowly).

 ## PRACTICE TIP

Both the 6th and octave intervals go from a line to a space or a space to a line on the staff. (It also helps to remember that the notes in the octave are quite far apart.) The 7th interval goes from a space to a space with two spaces in between or from a line to a line with two lines in between. Knowing this will help you recognize these intervals quickly when reading music.

Intervals

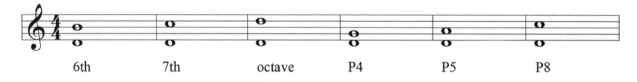

6th   7th   octave   P4   P5   P8

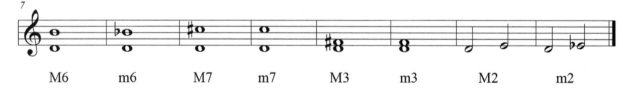

M6   m6   M7   m7   M3   m3   M2   m2

All major scales appear with fingerings on page 170.

One-Octave Scales

C MAJOR

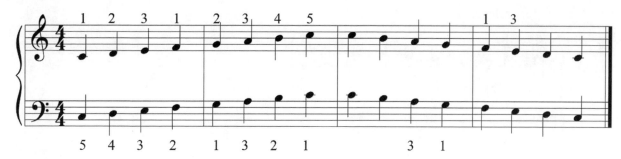

G MAJOR

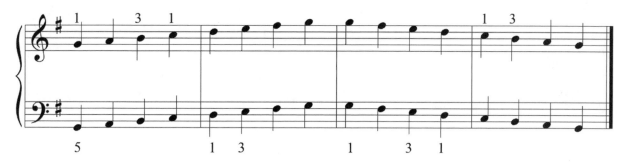

D MAJOR

🎼 PRACTICE TIP

The fingering that you learn for the D major scale in this lesson will be applied to numerous other scales, including C and G major.

There is no need to push yourself to play these scales hands together; there are very few instances (in all of the advanced piano literature) where one needs to play these scales hands together in parallel motion. But you will have to play a scale or parts of the scale one hand at a time, so practice these scales diligently.

Minor Romp

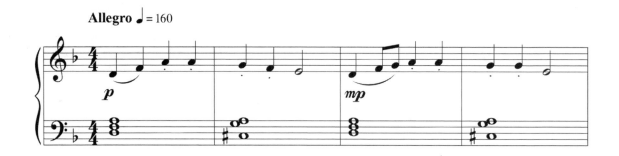

A "Türk-ish" Tune

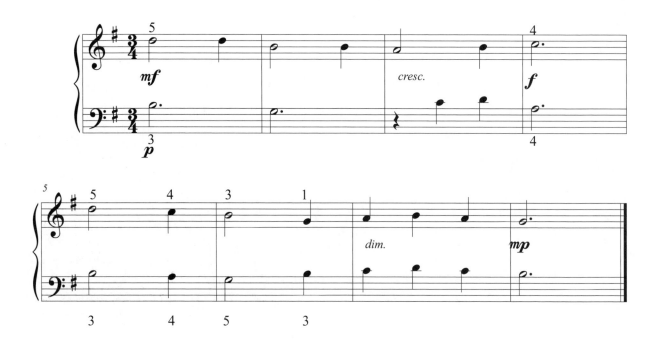

LESSON 16

Dotted Rhythms and Isolated Repetition

This lesson will focus on more musical details in some of the pieces you have been exposed to, including "Dance" by Diabelli, "Minor Romp," and "A 'Türk-ish' Tune." You will also check in on your scales, harmonize a new melody in D minor, and do a sight-reading example in G major. You will tap out the notes and rhythm for a famous minuet by Beethoven called Minuet in G. Finally, you will experiment with a new rhythm pattern called a dotted rhythm, as exemplified by "The Muffin Man."

KEY TERMS

ALLEGRO: Italian word that is a tempo marking for a fast, lively speed.

ANACRUSIS: A pickup note.

ANDANTE: Italian word that is a tempo marking for a walking pace.

DOTTED RHYTHMS: A rhythm with uneven or slightly unsteady notes.

MODERATO: Italian word that is a tempo marking for a moderate speed.

PRACTICE TIP

When you first start working on coordinating your hands to play together in a challenging piece, take it slower than you did when you played the piece with separate hands.

🎼 PRACTICE TIP

Think of practicing as musical triage: Prioritize the problems and then work down the list. Identify the top two or three worst problems, isolate them—being sure to choose a small enough section of music that you can fix in a relatively short amount of time—and then move to the next problem.

If you practice this way, you will make more efficient use of your time and won't be ingraining mistakes by playing them over and over. You will likely find that you need to rehearse these problem areas again at subsequent practice sessions, but hopefully you are able to fix them faster, and one day you'll sit down and these places won't be problems anymore.

PRACTICE ASSIGNMENT

❑ Play the G major scale [p. 61] with separate hands; use the long-short dotted rhythm pattern in the right hand.

❑ Review the major and minor finger patterns and chord progressions (in particular, review E minor because you will be playing in that key in the next lesson).

❑ Play "A 'Türk-ish' Tune" [p. 62] (try to finish learning and practice by isolating problem spots).

❑ Play the harmonization from this lesson [p. 65].

❑ Practice sight-reading [p. 65].

❑ Play "The Muffin Man" [p. 66] (right hand only).

❑ Tap out the notes and rhythm for the theme from Beethoven's Minuet in G Major [p. 66].

❑ Memorize the new tempo terms.

❑ Start coming up with a piano playlist—pieces that you'll have ready to perform or play at all times, even if that performance is only for yourself and not a public audience.

Harmonization

D MINOR ___ ___ ___ ___ ___ ___

DIRECTIONS FOR HARMONIZING THE MELODY

1   Play a block chord on beats 1 and 3 in each measure.

2   Where there is a line indicated, you will change your chord.

3   Write in your Roman numerals on each line below the staff.

4   Use inversion of your chords to make left hand movement easier.

TIPS FOR CHOOSING THE APPROPRIATE CHORD

When most melody notes are:

- D, F, or A, play the i chord.

- G, B♭, or D, play the iv chord.

- A, C♯, E, or G, play the V^7 chord.

Sight-Reading

The Muffin Man

English Song

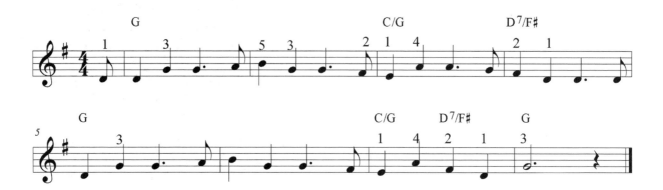

Theme from Minuet in G Major

Beethoven, WoO 10, No. 2
arr. Pike

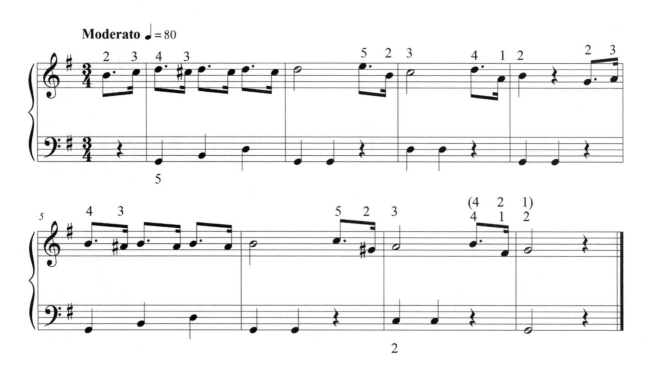

LESSON 17

Secondary Chords and More Dotted Rhythms

In this lesson, you will check in on the pieces from the previous lesson—including "A 'Türk-ish' Tune," "The Muffin Man," and Beethoven's Minuet in G—to assess what you should continue to work on, and you will learn a few new pieces: "A Beginning Piece," "Mournful Melody," and "Harp Étude." You will also harmonize "The Muffin Man" and learn the primary chord progression for E minor. In addition, you will continue to expand your theory knowledge by learning more about dotted rhythm patterns and exploring secondary chords. In particular, you will learn a new chord progression that includes one of the secondary chords, and the lesson will end with some more dotted rhythms in isolated measures of Minuet in G.

By this point in the course, you may feel like you have started to plateau in your piano learning. This is quite normal in many learning situations, but in this course, you are trying to acquire new musical knowledge, learn intricate technique and fine motor skills, and apply all of this new information in the new music that you practice.

Learning to play the piano is quite complex. During the past several lessons, you have learned several new, challenging piano techniques so that you can progress to the next level, and you may be experiencing mild frustration with some of the music. But don't give up. Keep practicing, and when you need a break, go back and revisit some of the music you learned in earlier lessons.

PASSING TONE: A nonchord tone that moves by step from one note of a chord to the next.

SECONDARY CHORDS: The four chords that are not primary chords but must go to a primary chord for resolution; the second, third, sixth, and seventh tones of the scale.

PRACTICE ASSIGNMENT

❑ Play the secondary progression in G (with correct left hand fingering); improvise a melody in the right hand and notate it below.

❑ Try to figure out the secondary chords in C and D major and play these on the piano.

❑ Play "The Muffin Man" [p. 66] (right hand as written; left hand blocked chords on beats 1 and 3).

❑ Play Beethoven's Minuet in G [p. 66] (right hand melody only).

❑ Play "A Beginning Piece" [p. 69].

❑ Play "Mournful Melody " [p. 69].

❑ Play "Harp Étude" [p. 70] (change pedal every two measures).

❑ Review any repertoire or music that still needs work.

Improvisation in G

A Beginning Piece

Mournful Melody

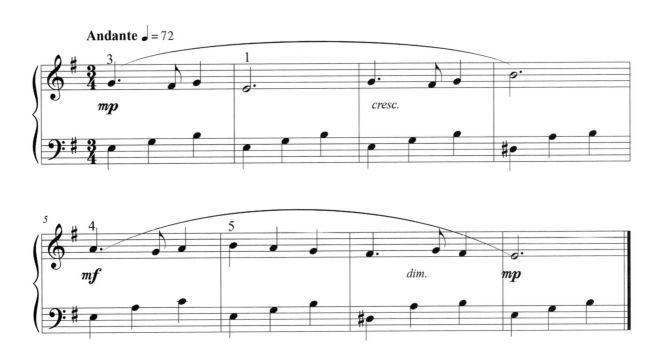

Harp Étude

legato

Ped.

LESSON 18

Sixteenth Notes and More Secondary Chords

In this lesson, you will review and refine some of the new music from the previous lesson, including "Mournful Melody," Beethoven's Minuet in G, "The Muffin Man," and "Harp Étude." You will also get a chance to play your improvisation with the minor ii chord, work with two of the other secondary chords that you learned in the previous lesson (the ii and vi chords), and learn about sixteenth notes in more detail. The lesson will end by previewing two sight-reading examples, one in the key of E minor and the other in G major.

> **F**ingering will not be included in more difficult piano scores. Instead, you will have to choose the fingering yourself. This is why you need to know not just what to do, but why a particular fingering choice is made.

KEY TERMS

EIGHTH NOTE: Rhythmic symbol that has a solid black head and a straight stem with one flag; held for half of a count, or beat.

SIXTEENTH NOTE: Rhythmic symbol that has a solid black head and a straight stem with two flags; held for a quarter of a count, or beat.

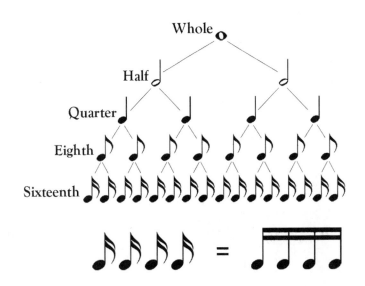

There are four different ways that music educators teach students to count out loud, but the only way to count in piano music—where each hand may have a different rhythm—is by using a normative system, which involves using numbers at the beginning of each beat and syllables to subdivide those beats. The numbers help you keep track of where you are in each measure, and you say the subdivisions for the smallest note in the piece, so you don't rush through longer notes.

PRACTICE ASSIGNMENT

- ☐ Warm up with your favorite 5-finger patterns and chord progressions (be sure to play E minor and the one-octave G major scale, because you are playing music in both of these keys this week).

- ☐ Play the secondary progression with ii and vi [below] (these chords will be used in new harmonization examples in the next lesson).

- ☐ Play Beethoven's Minuet [p. 66] (hands together; keep a steady beat; also practice right hand alone and count out loud).

- ☐ Review "Harp Étude" [p. 70] (with pedal).

- ☐ Practice sight-reading [p. 73].

 PRACTICE TIP

Don't underestimate the value of practicing left-hand blocking when your new music contains various types of left-hand accompaniment patterns. This practice will speed up your overall success with learning the piece.

Secondary Progression with ii and vi

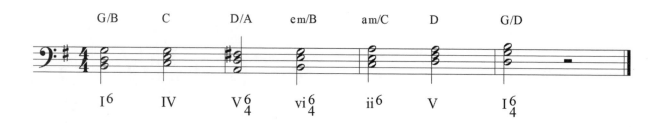

Sight-Reading

EXERCISE 1

EXERCISE 2

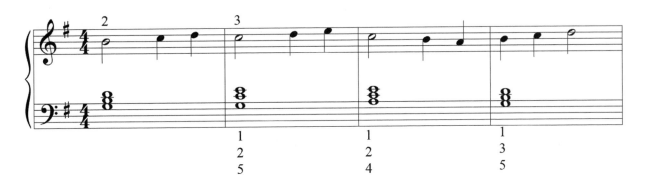

LESSON 19

Compound Meter and Technique

This lesson will begin with the two sight-reading exercises from the previous lesson and will review Beethoven's Minuet in G. Then, you will be introduced, measure by measure, to a new piece called "Cheerful Tune" that contains sixteenth notes and is played in the $\frac{2}{4}$ time signature, which you haven't played in yet. Next, you will play through the secondary chord progression with ii and vi that you've been practicing and learn how to harmonize the chords. You will also learn the difference between simple meter and compound meter and experience the $\frac{6}{8}$ time signature in a new piece called "Rocking Étude" (in E minor). Finally, you will be exposed to two technical exercises, both in a C major 5-finger pattern, that will help you strengthen your fingers and develop better hand coordination.

Almost every pianist on the planet has probably learned Hanon exercises at some point or another. However, they can increase tension in the hand and are often not played musically.

In contrast, the two technical exercises in this lesson—written by Cornelius Gurlitt as part of his opus 82—develop some of the same technical skills, but you'll be less likely to experience tension at this stage in the learning process.

KEY TERMS

COMMON TIME: See **QUADRUPLE METER**; sometimes represented by a " **C** " at the beginning of a piece instead of $\frac{4}{4}$.

COMPOUND METER: A class of meters in which each beat is subdivided into three sub-beats; typically has an 8 on the bottom of the time signature, which tells the kind of note that serves as the sub-beat, while the top number is usually 3, 6, or 9.

DUPLE METER: A meter that has two beats per measure, and each beat is a quarter-note long; represented as $\frac{2}{4}$.

QUADRUPLE METER: A meter that has four beats per measure, and each beat is a quarter-note long; represented as $\frac{4}{4}$.

SIMPLE METER: A class of meters in which each beat is subdivided into two sub-beats.

TRIPLE METER: A meter that has three beats per measure, and each beat is a quarter-note long; represented as $\frac{3}{4}$.

PRACTICE ASSIGNMENT

☐ Do "Technique 1" and "Technique 2" by Gurlitt [p. 76].

☐ Play "Cheerful Tune" [p. 76].

☐ Play "Rocking Étude" [p. 77].

☐ Play the harmonization from this lesson [p. 77] (figure out the chords first, then the right hand; you'll try it with both hands in the next lesson).

☐ Play Beethoven's Minuet in G [p. 66] (review for a few more days).

☐ Review some of your favorite music from past lessons.

 **PRACTICE TIP**

A practice technique for gradually speeding up a piece of music is to treat it like a game as you challenge yourself during practice.

Start with a practice tempo to work toward. As you become more confident during the week, check your metronome to see how close you are doing in comparison to the suggested tempo. It's okay if you aren't close. Just nudge up the metronome tempo a little each time, until you can no longer sustain the tempo and play accurately; then, nudge it back down a little and practice the piece at that tempo for a few more sessions. Once this slightly faster tempo becomes comfortable, you can use the metronome to push up until you can't keep up again.

Technique 1

Gurlitt Op. 82, No. 5

Technique 2

Gurlitt Op. 82, No. 9

Cheerful Tune

Rocking Étude

Rocking Gently

Harmonization

Folk Song

🎼 PRACTICE TIP

With lots of practice of music examples in various keys, you'll become quicker at finding chords and at moving your hand to each chord on the piano.

Some piano learners find that writing out the chords helps speed up the practice process. But if being able to play lead lines and harmonize melodies to familiar tunes is a goal of yours, then it is recommended that you do not write out the chords. Yes, each time you sit down to practice, you'll essentially have to figure out the chords again, but each time you practice, your chord identification will become faster and you will automate some steps in the process, even without realizing it.

LESSON 20

Parallel Major and Minor Keys

In this lesson, you will begin by playing "Technique 1," first with a moderate tempo and then in the key of D major. Then, you will play the full-octave scale in D major with the left hand. Next, you will explore the secondary chords of E minor and B minor with a chord progression and harmonization. You will also check on your progress with the harmonization from lesson 19, as well as play "Cheerful Tune" and "Rocking Étude." You will be introduced to an arrangement of a longer piece by Cornelius Gurlitt titled "Bell Melody" and another new piece titled "Elephant Stroll." Then, you will learn more about major and minor keys—specifically, parallel keys. Finally, you will play "Technique 2" from the previous lesson in the parallel minor mode and learn a 2-hand accompaniment, which involves playing chords in both hands (no melody): "G Major Broken Chord Accompaniment."

KEY TERM

PARALLEL KEYS: Keys whose key signatures are different but that share the same letter name (i.e., D major and D minor).

To make a major chord minor, lower the middle note by a half step.

PRACTICE TIP

Singing and playing piano at the same time can help you hear where to crescendo and diminuendo within each phrase.

PRACTICE ASSIGNMENT

- ❑ Play "Technique 1" and "Technique 2" [p. 76] (in C, G, D, and A major and C, G, D, and A minor).

- ❑ Play the harmonization from lesson 19 [p. 77].

- ❑ Play the harmonization from this lesson [below].

- ❑ Play "G Major Broken Chord Accompaniment" [below] with pedal .

- ❑ Play "Bell Melody" [p. 80].

- ❑ Play "Elephant Stroll" [p. 80].

Harmonization

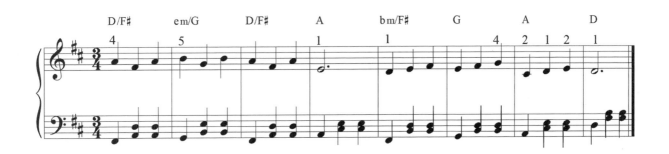

G Major Broken Chord Accompaniment

Ped.

Bell Melody

Gurlitt Op. 74, No. 7
arr. Pike

Elephant Stroll

LESSON 21

Three Forms of the Minor Scale and Syncopation

In this lesson, you will warm up with "Technique 2" from lesson 19 in the parallel minor key, and you will be introduced to a new piece that incorporates the major and minor modalities called "Major-Minor Mash-Up." Then, you will play "Technique 1" from lesson 19 in G minor and then in the parallel G major. Next, you will play the "G Major Broken Chord Accompaniment" from the previous lesson and then use that basic pattern to accompany a melody but with a more sophisticated rhythm, called a syncopated rhythm, for a piece called "Swing Low." You will also check on "Harmonization in D Major," "Bell Melody," and "Elephant Stroll" from the previous lesson. Then, you will explore the minor scale in more depth, which, unlike the major scale, has three different forms: the natural minor, harmonic minor, and melodic minor. Finally, you will be introduced to an arrangement of the main theme in Waltz in A Minor by Frédéric Chopin.

Take a moment to appreciate how far you've progressed in just a few short lessons. You've gone from reading very basic off-staff rhythms and pitches to much more complicated rhythmic patterns. You're also moving around the keyboard much more—by expanding and contracting your hand and through gentle shifts and leaps. You've also been playing music in major keys and minor keys.

KEY TERMS

HARMONIC MINOR: The form of the minor scale in which the seventh scale degree is raised by half a step on the way up and on the way down.

MELODIC MINOR: The form of the minor scale in which both the sixth and seventh scale degrees are raised by a half step on the ascent but are lowered on the descent.

NATURAL MINOR: The form of the minor scale that occurs when we start on the tonic and, moving up by step, play only the notes in the key signature.

SYNCOPATION: The action of playing or clapping on weaker beats and holding the note through the stronger beats.

Remember to do your warm-ups and cooldowns and be sure to stretch and take breaks, especially if you are spending longer at the piano these days.

Many people find it helpful to divide their practice into two shorter sessions and spread those throughout the day. For example, you might choose to do your main practice in the mornings, when your brain and body are fresh and well rested, and then do a shorter session in the evening to review and consolidate some of the learning from earlier in the day.

PRACTICE ASSIGNMENT

❑ Play these one-octave scales: C, G, D, and A major and A and D harmonic minor.

> Select harmonic minor scales appear with fingerings on page 173.

❑ Play "Technique 1" and "Technique 2" from lesson 19 [p. 76] in C, G, D, and A major and C, G, D, and A minor.

❑ Play the Waltz in A Minor theme [p. 83].

❑ Play "Major-Minor Mash-Up " [p. 84].

❑ Play the "Swing Low" 2-hand accompaniment [p. 85].

❑ Review music that still needs practice (or, if you need a break, play some of the easier pieces in your repertoire).

A Minor Scale

NATURAL

MELODIC

HARMONIC

Theme from Waltz in A Minor

Chopin
arr. Pike

Major-Minor Mash-Up

Vivace

Swing Low

Traditional
arr. Pike

> If you stumble when playing the "Swing Low" accompaniment, it can be difficult to jump back in. Because the instructor can't hear you, she can't wait for you if you make a mistake. This is actually a good thing, because continuing after stumbles is a critical skill for pianists to possess.
>
> After all, the orchestra conductor can't wait for the clarinetist if he or she flubs his or her notes; the band carries on and the player jumps back in.

LESSON 22

Artistic Expression and More Minor Keys

In this lesson, you will begin by playing the "Swing Low" accompaniment while the instructor plays the melody; because the accompaniment features a left hand that has to move faster than the right, this will help get your left hand involved in more complex rhythmic and melodic patterns. Then, you will learn a new piece, "Left Hand Legato Study," which also features a left-hand melody. Next, you will play the "Major-Minor Mash-Up," focusing on the musical expression and your dynamics. You will also play the A harmonic minor scale and Chopin's Waltz in A Minor. Then, you will be introduced to the E harmonic minor scale and a short piece that is in the key of E minor called "Melodic Dance." You will also be introduced to the B harmonic minor scale as well as the 5-finger patterns for C♯ and F♯ minor. Finally, you will be exposed to "Left Hand Octave Étude" to get you leaping the interval of an octave, which is very common in music.

KEY TERMS

CANTABILE: Italian word that musicians translate as "in a singing style"; it means to listen to your playing, try to shape your phrases, and (often) play legato.

PICARDY 3RD: A major 3rd in the final chord that ends a minor composition, rather than a minor 3rd; a very common technique in music.

SUBITO: Italian word that means "suddenly."

SUSPENSION: The creation of dissonance by prolonging a note (often across a bar line) that is part of the harmony from the previous measure while the new harmony begins; the dissonance is resolved by moving the dissonant note down by a step.

PRACTICE ASSIGNMENT

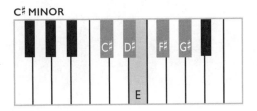

C# MINOR

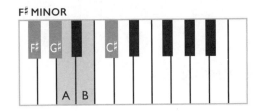

F# MINOR

☐ Practice the major and minor scales, especially A, D, and E harmonic minor and A major.

☐ Practice the minor 5-finger patterns (C# and F#; use legato or staccato articulation).

☐ Play the Waltz in A Minor theme [p. 83].

☐ Play "Swing Low" accompaniment with the recorded melody [p. 85].

☐ Learn the right hand of the B harmonic minor scale [p. 88].

☐ Play "Melodic Dance" [p. 88].

☐ Play "Left Hand Octave Étude" [p. 88].

☐ Play "Left Hand Legato Study" [p. 89].

 PRACTICE TIPS

≈ *When first trying to get a feel for a passage, it can be useful to play it with the correct fingering but not in rhythm.*

≈ *Often, students become distracted with anticipation when performing for a teacher, and the dynamics are the first thing that disappear from the performance. Thinking about and analyzing how dynamics are related to the musical line, form, or harmonic progression can really help you remember to include this important musical element when you play.*

≈ *When you see "subito" or crescendo/diminuendo signs coming in the score, you tend to anticipate the new dynamic in your playing. But try not to anticipate them; rather, begin the dynamic change when it is indicated in the music (not when you see it).*

You've been focused on so many pitches, rhythms, notes, and new concepts as you learn and practice your pieces each day. However, this week as you practice, think about the expressive quality of the music and about how you use the technique that you have learned to convey that expression.

B Minor Scale

HARMONIC

Melodic Dance

Left Hand Octave Étude

Left Hand Legato Study, op. 108, no. 12

Schytte

LESSON 23

The Classical Period and Fortepianos

In this lesson, you will begin by playing "Melodic Dance," assessing your playing and learning practice tips for typical problem spots. Then, you will play "Left Hand Octave Étude," assessing your playing and attending to a few details, and you will learn "Right Hand Octave Étude." Next, you will check on your progress with the right hand of the A major scale as well as with the "Left Hand Legato Study." Finally, you will learn a little history of both the classical period of music and the fortepiano. Along the way, you will be introduced to a new study called "Articulation Étude," two new scales (F major and B major), and the theme from one of Mozart's most iconic sonatas: Sonata in C Major.

KEY TERM

TENUTO: Italian word meaning "to hold"; the mark indicates to hold the note for its full value or can be a weak accent mark; notated with a line above or below the notehead ($\bar{\rho}\ \bar{\downarrow}$).

PRACTICE ASSIGNMENT

❑ Practice the major and minor scales, especially A, D, E, and B harmonic minor and A, F, and B major.

❑ Review Waltz in A Minor [p. 83], "Left Hand Octave Étude" [p. 88], and "Left Hand Legato Study" [p. 89].

❑ Play "Right Hand Octave Étude" [p. 91].

❑ Play "Articulation Étude" [p. 91].

❑ Play the theme from Mozart's Sonata in C [p. 92] (4 measures only).

A Major Scale

(right hand only)

Right Hand Octave Étude

(slide)

Articulation Étude

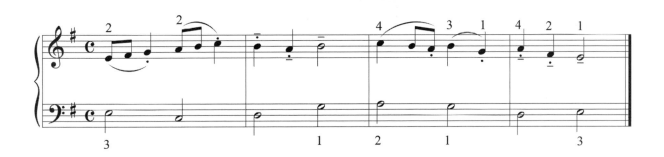

Sonata

Mozart
arr. Pike

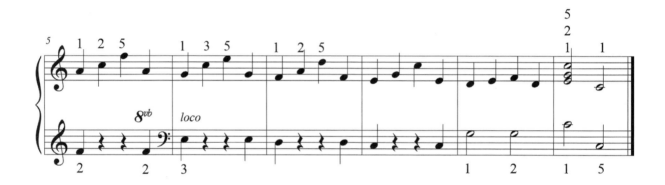

LESSON 24

Seventh Chords and Sonata Form

In this lesson, you will begin by playing your octave études. First, you will play "Left Hand Octave Étude" from lesson 22 and then transpose it into the key of D major. Second, you will play "Left Hand Octave Étude" from the previous lesson and assess your performance, especially listening for rhythmic consistency. Third, you will play "Articulation Étude" from the previous lesson, comparing your legato, staccato, detached, and tenuto articulation to the instructor's. Then, you will learn, measure by measure, an arrangement of Franz Joseph Haydn's German Dance in D Major. Next, you will learn about an important musical form in the classical period called the sonata form, and you will be introduced to Mozart's Sonata in C. You will also learn, measure by measure, a piece called "Carefree" that employs a left-hand Alberti bass pattern, which became codified in the classical period. Finally, you will discover the various types of 7th chords that are used in classical pieces.

Franz Joseph Haydn (1732–1809) was an important figure in the development and evolution of the classical music style. During his lifetime, he witnessed the birth and development of the classical style and even heard how composers like Beethoven were pushing the boundaries that eventually led to a new style of music. Haydn wrote masses, oratorios, songs for voice and keyboard, more than 100 symphonies, concerti, almost 70 string quartets, lots of other chamber works, and dozens of keyboard sonatas. He also wrote an inordinate number of pieces for the baryton, a bowed instrument that was similar to a modern cello. For the piano, he wrote a number of German Dances, and these are some of the first pieces by Haydn that students learn to play.

Because classical composers were trying to bring clarity to their music, most of the harmonies in classical pieces are primary and secondary chords. They also used various kinds of 7th chords, or four-note chords.

In addition to the dominant 7th, there are four other types of 7th chords. By simply changing the type of triad that is played in the bottom three notes and the type of 7th that is played between the bottom and the top notes, pianists create very different sounding 7th chords.

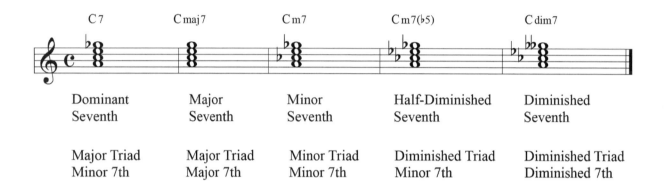

C 7	C maj7	C m7	C m7(♭5)	C dim7
Dominant Seventh	Major Seventh	Minor Seventh	Half-Diminished Seventh	Diminished Seventh
Major Triad Minor 7th	Major Triad Major 7th	Minor Triad Minor 7th	Diminished Triad Minor 7th	Diminished Triad Diminished 7th

KEY TERMS

7TH CHORD: A four-note chord consisting of a triad and a 7th interval.

DEVELOPMENT: The second section in sonata form, in which the composer develops one or more of the themes from the exposition.

DOUBLE FLAT (♭♭): A whole step below the original note; represented by two flat signs.

DOUBLE SHARP (×): A whole step above the original note.

EXPOSITION: The first section in sonata form, in which the themes are introduced.

MODULATION: The act of moving from one key and firmly establishing a new key within a piece.

RECAPITULATION: The third section in sonata form, in which the exposition is recapped.

SONATA: A multimovement work (usually consisting of three or four movements).

SONATINA: A short sonata.

A feature of the classical period was a revival of classic Greek forms, including simplicity and balance. In music, there were no extant musical examples from which to draw, so composers and theorists sought to create formal structures and predicable harmonic and cadential patterns that did away with some excesses of the previous era.

One of the most important forms, especially for pianists, that developed during the classical period was the sonata-allegro form, which these days is most commonly referred to simply as the sonata form.

A sonata is a multimovement work, usually with three or four movements. In three-movement sonatas, the first movement was fast, the second movement was slower, and the third movement was usually fast again. In four-movement sonatas, one of the middle movements could be a dance, such as the minuet and trio. The first movement of most sonatas and symphonies follow a particular form with three sections:

1 the exposition, which is where the themes are introduced;

2 the development, in which the composer develops one or more of these themes; and

3 the recapitulation, in which the exposition is recapped.

These same sections are also in shorter piano sonatinas, but there may only be one theme present in a sonatina.

Typically, in the exposition, the composer will introduce two themes: The first is in the tonic key while the second is in the dominant key. The development section usually begins in the new key. It is in this section that the composer will choose one or more of the themes from the exposition to develop. Essentially, the composer elaborates on and changes the theme in this section. A theme can be developed by changing pitches or modifying the rhythm—or both. Some composers also explored these themes by modulating to other keys.

By the late classical period, the development sections of sonata form became very long and complex. In sonatinas, the development section tends to be quite short.

Following the development, the composer will return to the first theme, though this is usually now played in the dominant key. In some sonatas and in concerti, there is a cadenza that features virtuosic playing by the soloist that signals the return to the opening theme. When the cadenza ends, the piece is at the beginning of the recapitulation. Because the piece has to end in the home key, the second theme in the recapitulation will be in the tonic.

PRACTICE ASSIGNMENT

- ❑ Practice any scales and warm-ups that you'd like to review.

- ❑ Play "Articulation Étude" [p. 91].

- ❑ Play the theme from Mozart's Sonata in C [p. 92] (4 measures).

- ❑ Play "Carefree" [below].

- ❑ Play Haydn's German Dance in D Major [p. 97] (first half only; separate hands for several days and then try slowly, hands together).

Carefree

German Dance

Haydn
arr. Pike

LESSON 25

Sight-Reading and Technique

In this lesson, you will begin by playing "Articulation Étude" and evaluating your progress. Then, you will play "Carefree," focusing on each hand's notes as well as the musical and expressive aspects of the piece. Next, you will be introduced to three new sight-reading examples; the third example has two additional exercises (harmonization and improvisation) to practice in conjunction with it. You will also encounter a new technique exercise by Gurlitt in the key of C major. Then, you will work on the theme from Mozart's Sonata in C. Finally, you will learn the second half of Haydn's German Dance in D Major, the first half of which you were introduced to in the previous lesson.

KEY TERM

PEDAL TONE: A single bass note from the harmony that is held through numerous measures, even when that note isn't part of the chord.

PRACTICE ASSIGNMENT

❑ Practice these scales: C, D, and A major and C, D, and A harmonic minor.

❑ Play the theme from Mozart's Sonata in C [p. 92] (more will be added in the future, so play this often enough to remain familiar with the notes).

❑ Play "Carefree" [p. 96] (listen for musical expression).

❑ Play Haydn's German Dance in D Major [p. 97] (second half).

❑ Play the technical exercise from this lesson [p. 99].

❑ Practice sight-reading [p. 100].

❏ Try the the following with the third sight-reading exercise [p. 100].

❏ Harmonization: Play exercise 3 with a waltz-style or broken-chord left hand pattern.

❏ Improvisation: Improvise your own melody (in D harmonic or D melodic minor) over the notated bass line.

 PRACTICE TIP

You should probably not let too much time pass without playing older scales or you could forget some of them and lose some of your dexterity and muscle memory. Be sure to check in on your primary chord progressions, too.

Because we are creatures of habit and many of us tend to play our favorite scales as warm-ups, you might find it helpful to create a list of all your scales in a separate notebook and jot down the date as you practice each one. Then, with a quick visual scan, you can see which scales or chords you've been neglecting.

Technical Exercise

Sight-Reading

EXERCISE 1

EXERCISE 2

EXERCISE 3

LESSON 26

The Romantic Period and Seventh-Chord Arpeggios

In this lesson, you will begin with the technique exercise from the previous lesson, isolating the measures and playing them slowly so that you have an opportunity to control your finger action. Then, you will play "Sight-Reading 1" from lesson 25, focusing on playing with the correct balance between the melody and the accompaniment as well as on experimenting with the dynamics. Next, you will play the sight-reading that you practiced for this lesson. You will also learn, measure by measure, a long repertoire piece: Johannes Brahms's Lullaby. Then, you will learn a little about the Romantic period of music. And because you will need to be able to play arpeggios for some Romantic works, you will begin learning some 7th-chord arpeggios in this lesson—specifically by exploring four major-minor 7th chords and playing them as arpeggios with the left hand. Finally, you will check on your progress with Haydn's German Dance from lesson 24.

PRACTICE ASSIGNMENT

- ☐ Practice these scales: G, D, and A major and D and A harmonic minor.

- ☐ Practice the technique exercise from lesson 25 [p. 99] (speed up this week).

- ☐ Practice 7th-chord arpeggios [p. 102].

 PRACTICE TIP

If a composer wrote something twice, play it differently each time as the performer. There's no hard-and-fast rule for how you do this, but if the phrase or motive is loud the first time, you could play it more softly the second time, treating the repetition as a kind of echo. Alternatively, you could play the first iteration of the motive softly and play louder, or more insistently, the second time.

- ❑ Play Haydn's German Dance in D Major [p. 97] (second half; hands together).

- ❑ Play "Carefree" [p. 96] (this isn't played in this lesson, but you will check on it in the next lesson, so be sure to review it).

- ❑ Play Brahms's Lullaby [p. 103] (hands separately).

- ❑ Finally, remember the two new rules for beginning pieces at the appropriate tempo and for playing repeated passages with dynamic contrast.

7th Chord Arpeggios

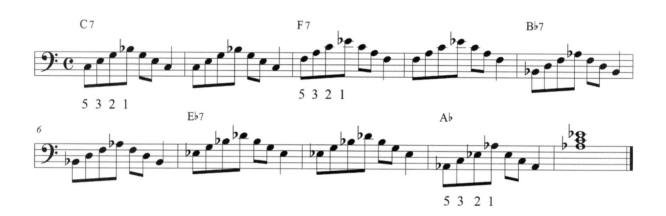

🎼 PRACTICE TIP

You can only play a piece as fast as you can play the most difficult part. Sometimes the tricky part is an entire section; other times it's only a measure. But most often, the beginning of the composition isn't as difficult and you'll know it really well (thus, you'll be inclined to play too quickly when you begin).

Before you begin to play the piece, think about the difficult spot and hear a little of it in your mind to ensure that you begin the piece at the slower tempo. If you aren't able to hear the music in your head just yet, that's normal; just play the tricky passage. Then, you'll have no doubt about how fast (or slow) you need to play the piece.

By doing this little trick, you'll be much more likely to maintain a consistent tempo throughout your entire performance. Of course, the ultimate objective is to improve the problem spot through practice so that you can play at your goal tempo.

Lullaby

Brahms
arr. Pike

LESSON 27

Extended Arpeggios and Pianist as Artist

The previous lesson ended with Haydn's German Dance; in this lesson, you will dive deeper into the second half. In the previous lesson, you also worked on the left hand of Brahms's Lullaby; in this lesson, you will add the pedal and start working on the right hand. In addition, because playing virtuosic arpeggios will become more important with Romantic repertoire, you will work on extended arpeggios—specifically the fingering for two-octave arpeggios—as well as review the 7th-chord arpeggios from the previous lesson. Then, you will learn a new piece called "The Harp," which has sweeping arpeggios that are shared between the hands. Next, you will review the left-hand B major scale. Finally, you will be introduced to two black-key scales: D♭ and G♭. While they do contain white keys, they begin on black keys, which is why they are labeled as black-key scales.

PRACTICE ASSIGNMENT

- ❏ Practice these two-octave arpeggios (separate hands): D, A, and E major.

- ❏ Practice the D♭ and G♭ major octave scales and the A♭ major 5-finger pattern.

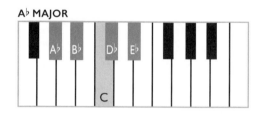

A♭ MAJOR

- ❏ Play Haydn's German Dance in D Major [p. 97] (hands together, focus on the first half; review the second half; slow tempo is okay).

- ❏ Play Brahms's Lullaby [p. 103] (hands together).

- ❏ Play "The Harp" [p. 105].

- ❏ Review older music or technical exercises.

> All major two-octave arpeggios appear with fingerings on page 175.

PRACTICE TIP

If you work through Haydn's German Dance in D Major in the following way, you will learn the first half with both hands before you know it. (This practice technique won't work for every piece, but it does work well for this one.)

- *Play measure 1 and stop on the downbeat of measure 2. Then, repeat that several more times until you're confident. Next, jump to measure 3 and, making sure that you begin with the correct finger on each note, play to the downbeat of measure 4. Then, do the same with measure 5 into 6 and 7 into 8.*

- *With this type of additive practice, you're ensuring that you don't pause at the bar line, but you're also becoming confident and feeling grounded on the downbeat of each measure.*

- *Then, go back and fill in the scale-type runs. In this piece, that means you play measures 1 and 2 and stop on the downbeat of measure 3. Once you have that, begin on the downbeat of measure 3 and play to the downbeat of measure 5. At this point, you can link those two spots together, playing measure 1 to the downbeat of measure 5. Just be sure to take your time and pace yourself.*

The Harp

LESSON 28

More Romantic Repertoire

In this lesson, you will begin by playing a piece that combines some of the arpeggio technique with musical expression—"The Harp" from the previous lesson—focusing first on the pitches and clean pedaling and then on the musical expression in this piece. Then, you will play Brahms's Lullaby (from lesson 26), focusing first on pitches, rhythms, and pedaling and then on dynamics. You will also be introduced to another harmonization example, in which the melody is in whole notes for the entire piece. Finally, you will be exposed to an arrangement of a Romantic masterpiece written by Franz Liszt called "Liebesträum"—your first major black-key piece—and you will be tasked with learning it, one measure at a time.

Franz Liszt (1811–1886) was a virtuosic pianist, which is reflected in his compositions. He changed the piano recital forever—not just with his virtuosity, but by being the first pianist to perform complete programs of piano music by himself and the first pianist to perform from memory. Both of these innovations remain part of the piano performance tradition today.

In 1844, Liszt settled in Weimar and became known as a great teacher. In fact, from 1871 until the end of his life, he divided his time between teaching and performing in Weimar, Paris, and Budapest. In his later years, his teaching took place in a group setting, much like a modern-day master class. Students who were accepted into his studio would gather at the appointed time and he would decide which pieces he wanted to teach that day. Then, the student would perform and have a lesson with the other students watching on and learning by listening.

KEY TERMS

RITARDANDO: Italian word indicating to become gradually slower, abbreviated rit.

RUBATO: Italian word meaning "to steal" or "to rob time"; the practice of pushing forward with the tempo and lingering slightly before regaining some speed without changing the basic pulse; common during the Romantic era.

PRACTICE ASSIGNMENT

☐ Practice these two-octave arpeggios (separate hands): D, A, and E major.

☐ Practice these one-octave scales (separate hands): G and D major.

☐ Play the theme from Mozart's Sonata in C [p. 92] (more will be added to it soon).

☐ Play Haydn's German Dance in D Major [p. 97].

☐ Play the harmonization example from this lesson [below] (your goal is to play this with an Alberti bass pattern in the left hand).

☐ Play "The Harp" [p. 108] (with dynamics and rubato).

☐ Play Brahms's Lullaby [p. 109] (hands together with dynamics).

☐ Play "Liebesträum" [p. 110] (separate hands this week; focus on the left hand chords).

Harmonization

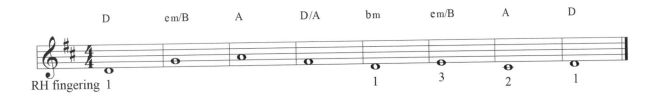

❧ If you hear any blurriness when using the pedal while playing a piece, lift your foot a little sooner. If the pedal does not sound as though it is helping you connect one chord to the next, you are lifting your foot too soon—this tends to be the more common problem.

❧ As you gain more control over your fingers, achieving just the right dynamic level will become easier, but for now, listen carefully to the dynamic level that you are producing, try to adjust as you practice, and be patient with yourself. If you are having trouble hearing your dynamics, record yourself and listen back. Don't be too harsh of a critic when you listen to the recording because things don't always sound as we think they do!

The Harp

(with dynamics)

Lullaby

(with dynamics)

Brahms
arr. Pike

Liebesträum

Liszt
arr. Pike

LESSON 29

Sonata Form Revisited

In this lesson, you will begin by reviewing Brahms's Lullaby, including as many of the dynamic contrasts as you can and listening carefully to your pedaling and to the melody. Then, you will play "The Harp," including the dynamics and the rubato as you play. Next, you will be introduced to a new piece: Waltz in C by the Romantic composer Cornelius Gurlitt. You will also review the harmonization from the previous lesson, comparing your notes to the instructor's to ensure that you've learned it correctly. Then, you will be introduced to another new piece by Gurlitt called "Mini-Sonatina," whose sonata form is modified; instead of two themes, there is really only one theme, but it is played twice. You previously learned the first part of the theme from Mozart's Sonata in C; in this lesson, you will be exposed to an arrangement of the rest of this theme. Finally, you will check on your progress with Liszt's "Liebestraüm" and try to play it hands together.

KEY TERM

LOCO: Italian word meaning to play as written; indication often seen following a passage where your hand has been displaced by an octave as a reminder to no longer play at that octave and to resume playing as written on the staff.

PRACTICE ASSIGNMENT

❑ Warm-up 1: Play the harmonization from lesson 28 with Alberti bass [p. 107].

❑ Warm-up 2: Play "The Harp" [p. 108] or arpeggios of your choice; just remember that if you play "The Harp" as a warm-up piece, play it musically.

- ❑ Play "Liebesträum" [p. 110] (hands together; goal tempo: eighth note = 80).

- ❑ Play Gurlitt's Waltz in C [below] (measures 1–16 separate hands).

- ❑ Play "Mini-Sonatina" [p. 114] (slowly, hands together).

- ❑ Play the theme from Mozart's Sonata in C [p. 92] (add the new part, which is the end of theme 1).

- ❑ Keep Haydn's German Dance [p. 97] on your list, as you will return to it soon!

As your music becomes more complex and difficult, it may take several weeks to learn and perfect an entire piece. This is normal, so don't feel as though you are the only person who has ever struggled to learn challenging music. In fact, when you hear people say that musicians have discipline, a big part of what they've developed is persistence to continue learning difficult music over an extended period of time. So, remember to be patient with yourself and keep breaking down your big goals into more manageable objectives that you can meet each week between lessons.

Waltz in C

Gurlitt
arr. Pike

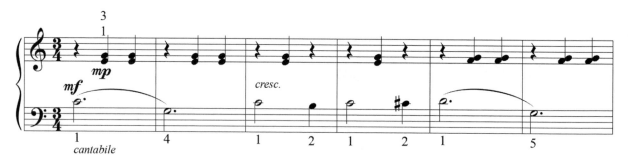

Mini-Sonatina

Gurlitt
arr. Pike

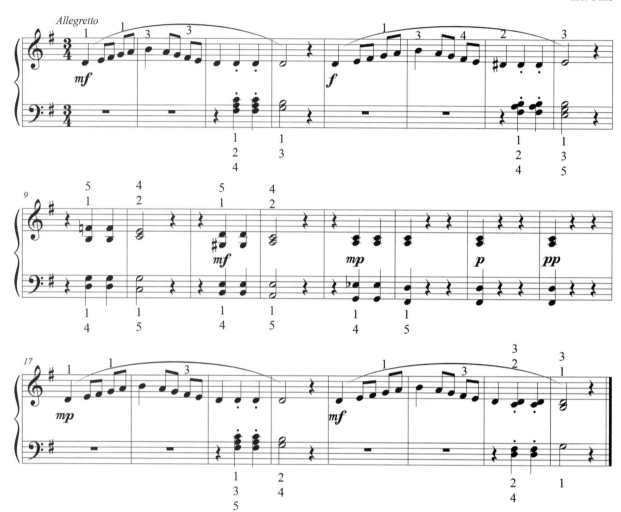

LESSON 30

The Baroque Era and Harpsichords

In this lesson, you will get your fingers moving with the harmonization from lesson 28 and then play the theme from Mozart's Sonata in C Major, especially checking on your progress with the new part from the previous lesson. Next, you will play "Mini-Sonatina," with a focus on the dynamics. You will also play the first half of Gurlitt's Waltz in C, which you started learning in the previous lesson, as well as learn the second half of the piece. Then, you will begin exploring the baroque era. You will also play Haydn's German Dance from lesson 24. Finally, you will be tasked with previewing a new baroque piece—Jean-Philippe Rameau's Minuet—on your own before the next lesson.

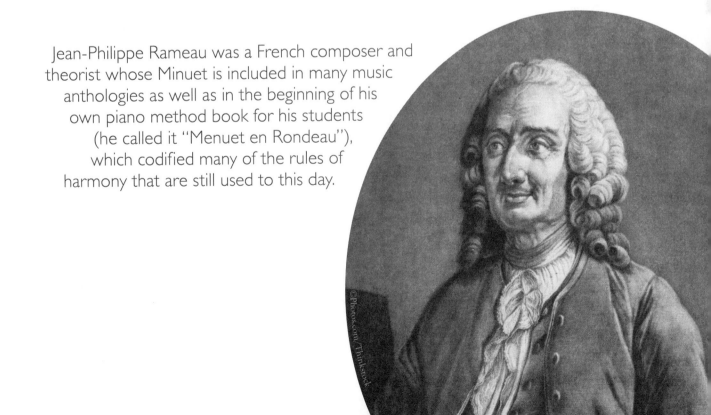

Jean-Philippe Rameau was a French composer and theorist whose Minuet is included in many music anthologies as well as in the beginning of his own piano method book for his students (he called it "Menuet en Rondeau"), which codified many of the rules of harmony that are still used to this day.

Keyboard music began to flourish during the baroque period and was primarily performed on the organ, harpsichord, or clavichord. Although Bartolomeo Christofori invented the piano before the baroque era ended, it did not come into its own until the classical era.

Harpsichords and clavichords were less substantial instruments, in terms of size and weight, than the fortepiano or modern piano. There were fewer octaves of keys on the keyboard, and their sound was quite different from the piano. In fact, in part because they could sustain less tension from the strings, the tuning was different from modern tuning. Harpsichords and violins were tuned to a lower-sounding pitch than modern instruments are today. Also, during the early part of the baroque era, tuning varied depending on the key of the composition.

In terms of tone production, on the harpsichord, tone was produced when plectra (little picks that were often made of quills or leather) plucked each string. The entire mechanism is quite noisy. On clavichords, a piece of metal, often a brass blade, struck each string when a key was depressed; it produced a relatively soft sound, in spite of the metal blade.

KEY TERMS

CONTRAPUNTAL MUSIC: Music that uses counterpoint.

COUNTERPOINT: The practice of playing two or more melodic lines simultaneously, rather than having a single melody accompanied by chords.

TRIO SONATA: A form of the multimovement sonata that has three different staves of music on the written scores, but—although it sounds like there would be three players—such sonatas actually required four performers (usually two unspecified solo instruments, a bass player, and a keyboardist who realized or improvised an accompaniment based on the figured bass).

PRACTICE ASSIGNMENT

❑ Review one scale and one chord progression each time you practice and choose an older piece as a warm-up for your fingers.

❑ Play Gurlitt's Waltz in C [p. 112] (measures 1–16 hands together; measures 17–34 separate hands).

- Play "Mini-Sonatina" [p. 114] (hands together with dynamics; goal tempo: quarter note = 112).

- Finish learning "Liebesträum" [p. 110].

- Play Rameau's Minuet [below] (try to learn four measures of the right hand before the next lesson; follow all of the fingering closely).

- Review any repertoire from previous lessons.

Minuet

Rameau
arr. Pike

LESSON 31

Baroque Repertoire

This lesson will begin by reviewing Gurlitt's Waltz in C and "Mini-Sonatina," gradually speeding up both pieces as well as incorporating dynamic contrasts into both. Then, you will learn, measure by measure, the new piece from your previous practice assignment: Rameau's Minuet, which you will be tasked to learn, hands separately, before the next lesson. Next, you will be exposed to another piece from the baroque era: Johann Pachelbel's Canon, which contains a compositional device called a ground bass that was important during the baroque era. This piece was originally written in a different key, but it is arranged in C major to make it easier for you to play for now. Finally, you will be introduced to a new harmonization example—a Ukrainian folk song in E minor, which will offer you a chance to review the key of E minor and practice playing accompaniment patterns.

KEY TERMS

DA CAPO: Italian phrase that means "the head."

D.C. AL FINE: An indication to go back to the head—D.C. stands for da capo, which means "the head"—of the piece (the top of the piece, or the beginning) and play until you see the "fine" sign.

FINE: Italian word that means "finish" or "ending."

FUGUE: A contrapuntal piece in which there is a theme called a subject—which is introduced in several voices, both at the original pitch and in transposed versions—as well as a theme known as the answer to the subject.

Although there were works called sonatas during the baroque era, they really didn't resemble the sonata that became one of the most important instrumental forms during the classical era.

GROUND BASS: A bass line that is repeated over and over throughout a piece.

RONDEAU: A French musical and poetic form from the 14th and 15th centuries; also popular in French harpsichord music of the baroque era; features a refrain that returns between subsidiary sections.

RONDO: A musical form with five or more sections featuring a recurring main section (i.e., ABACA).

Waltzes are characterized by a strong pulse on the downbeat, so they are actually easier to play and sound better if they are played quickly.

PRACTICE ASSIGNMENT

- ❏ Practice the E harmonic minor one-octave scale and the E minor primary chord progression, as these will help you with the new harmonization example.

- ❏ Play the C and G major one-octave scales and primary chord progressions in C and G major.

- ❏ Play Gurlitt's Waltz in C [p. 112] (hands together; listen for balance and dynamics; goal tempo: quarter note = 160).

- ❏ Play "Mini-Sonatina" [p. 114].

- ❏ Play Rameau's Minuet [p. 117] (separate hands for four days, then try hands together).

- ❏ Play the harmonization exercise from this lesson [p. 120] (follow the instructions and prepare both hands).

- ❏ Play Pachelbel's Canon [p. 120] (separate hands; try to do the dynamics indicated on the score).

 PRACTICE TIP

Although you will likely need to keep working on some of these baroque pieces for five or six days of practice, hopefully you are up for the challenge. Just remember to listen to the harmonies and the sounds that you are producing at the piano as you practice. It can be very easy to get so caught up with the mechanical and technical aspects of the repertoire that you forget to listen to the beautiful music.

Harmonization

DIRECTIONS FOR HARMONIZING THE MELODY

1 Practice the melody first.

2 Practice with half-note blocked chords in the left hand.

3 Practice with quarter-note "oom-pah" chords in the left hand.

Canon

Pachelbel
arr. Pike

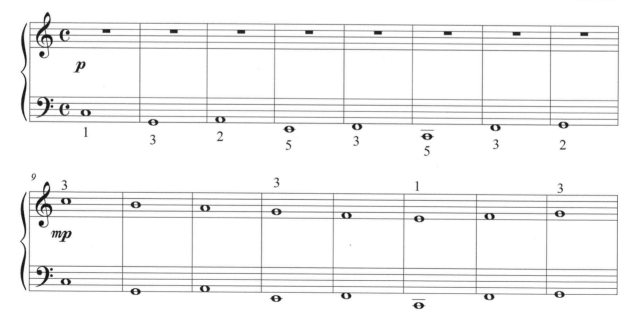

LESSON 32

Deliberate Practice and Learning Music

This lesson will begin with a warm-up that includes the E harmonic minor scale and the E minor primary chord progression. Then, you will begin working on the harmonization example that was introduced at the end of the previous lesson, which is in the key of E minor. Next, you will play the longest piece that you've learned so far: Gurlitt's Waltz, which you have been working on playing with both hands and at a faster tempo. Try to keep both hands going and focus on bringing out the melody; your goal is to experience the joy of playing this piece at an allegro speed. Then, you will learn a few new technical exercises that are designed to help you refine your finger action and to gain a little more independence between your fingers; focus on your fingers, trying to stay relaxed yet playing each finger with about the same amount of firmness. Finally, you will review Rameau's Minuet.

KEY TERM

DELIBERATE PRACTICE: Also called self-regulation, practice that involves three steps: forethought, volitional control, and self-evaluation/reflection.

PRACTICE ASSIGNMENT

☐ Play Gurlitt's Waltz in C [p. 112] (goal tempo: quarter note = 160).

☐ Play Rameau's Minuet [p. 117] (hands together; dynamics; balance).

☐ Play Pachelbel's Canon [p. 120] (hands together).

❑ Review the harmonization example from lesson 31 [p. 120].

❑ Play the technique exercises "Flying Fingers" (right hand only) and "Low-Flying Fingers" [p. 123] (goal tempo for the next lesson: quarter note = 104).

Flying Fingers

Low-Flying Fingers

DELIBERATE PRACTICE

Psychologists and music educators alike are very interested in musicians and their practice. There are two related aspects that researchers study: how much and what kind of practice is required to become an expert in a field, and what expert musicians do during practice.

With respect to the first aspect, there is a specific kind of practice called deliberate practice, or self-regulation, that is required to achieve mastery in any field. But in highly specialized areas, such as music performance, deliberate practice is critical, and there is quite a bit of data to support the notion that it takes about 10 years or 10,000 hours of deliberate practice to become an expert.

Researchers have learned a great deal about self-regulation, or deliberate practice, by studying experts in various fields, and pianists seem to be a favored group to observe for research purposes. There are essentially three steps involved in deliberate practice:

1   Forethought, which involves choosing an appropriate and specific objective or goal for the practice session;

2   Volitional control, which involves our ability to assess what and how we are doing as we work on the specific task and to remain flexible and choose appropriate strategies to meet the specific objective; and

3   Self-evaluation, or reflection, which is both ongoing during the practicing task—to know whether strategies are working and if musical goals are being met—but also occurs at the conclusion of the practice session, as one reflects on what worked well and begins to articulate new goals and objectives for the next practice session.

Although there are three steps to self-regulation, they aren't necessarily linear. One does have to use forethought to devise appropriate goals, but there is a good deal of reflection and self-evaluation going on during the volitional control phase. And if goals are met, new goals could be conceived of and worked on during the practice session. The process can be viewed as more of a spiral—as one identifies problems, tries strategies, listens, and evaluates—rather than a straight line from a to b.

It turns out that deliberate practice takes practice. But that's what you've been encouraged to do from the first lesson of this course. You've had to take ownership of your listening and evaluation, write practice strategies and reminders for yourself in your music, and compare your performances to the instructor's ideal version. Since the beginning of this course, you've been learning to self-regulate, so keep developing your self-regulation and deliberate practice skills during each practice session.

It's okay to just sit down and run through or play your repertoire; in fact, practicing performing it this way can be both enjoyable and helpful before a lesson. But playing through your music is not deliberate practice, and without deliberate practice, you will not progress as expeditiously as you might otherwise.

LESSON 33

The 20th Century and Modern Music

In this lesson, you will begin by playing all the way through Gurlitt's Waltz at the goal tempo from your previous practice. Then, you will play one of the finger exercises that you were introduced to in the previous lesson, "Flying Fingers," which will prepare your fingers for Rameau's Minuet, which you will play with both hands all the way through. Next, you will check on another challenging piece of baroque repertoire: Pachelbel's Canon. You will also be exposed to a new harmonization that will require your left hand to move, so you will play "Low-Flying Fingers" and then preview "Lavender's Blue" in the key of G major. You will also learn, measure by measure, a piece that features broken chords called "Ode to Schumann," which is a nod to Romantic composer Robert Schumann. Then, you will be introduced to the period of music called modern or contemporary music, written in the 20th and 21st centuries. Finally, you will learn a piece called "The Tower Keeper" that includes a few modern compositional techniques for the piano.

KEY TERMS

12-TONE TECHNIQUE: Technique of writing music in which all 12 pitches in an octave are assigned a number (called a tone row) and each has to be used before the composer can reuse a pitch.

ALEATORY: Music that leaves some elements to chance (i.e., there might be instructions for the performer to choose a unique rhythm, or set of pitches, which could be played in any order or improvised during performance).

ATONAL: Music that avoids musical tonality.

POLYRHYTHM: Rhythm that contains different rhythmic patterns played simultaneously.

PROGRAMMATIC MUSIC: Type of music in which a picture or story is conveyed through the instrumental composition.

- ❑ Play the technique exercises "Flying Fingers" (hands together) and "Low-Flying Fingers" [p. 123] (goal tempo: quarter note = 104).

- ❑ Play "Lavender's Blue" [p. 128] (harmonization, playing broken chords in the left hand).

- ❑ Play "Ode to Schumann" [below] (hands together; slowly; try to use suggested fingering).

- ❑ Play "The Tower Keeper" [p. 129] (have fun knocking on the piano and exploring different ways to create sound at the keyboard, if you have an acoustic piano).

- ❑ Review Rameau's Minuet [p. 117] or Pachelbel's Canon [p. 120].

In reality, there are many different styles represented in all of the music that has been written during the 20th and 21st centuries, but in this course, this music is called modern or contemporary.

Ode to Schumann

CONTINUED

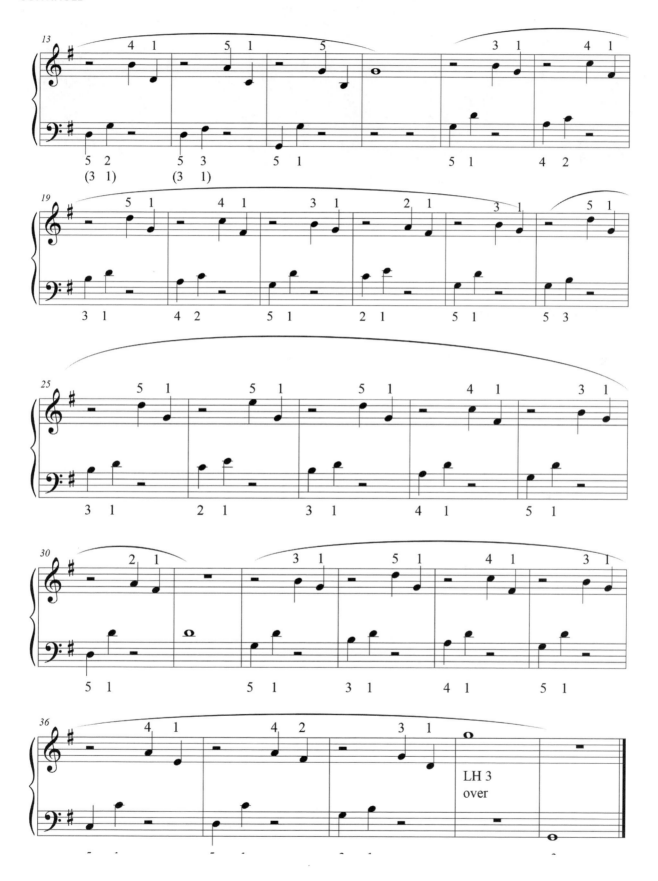

Lavender's Blue

English Folk Song
arr. Pike

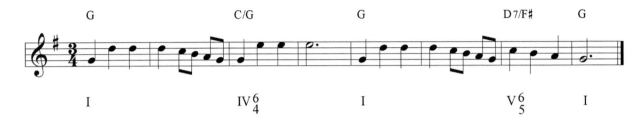

 PRACTICE TIPS

≈ *If you can't manage to reach the goal tempo of a piece as played in a lesson, it may be an unrealistic tempo for that particular stage in your learning and you may wish to continue working toward the goal on your own. Or you may set the piece aside for a while and come back to it after you've gained some more experience with playing the piano. Teachers and pianists will sometimes let repertoire "rest" for a while. While you don't want to set every challenging piece aside, sometimes it helps to give the music an incubation period while you work on other material. You will be continuing to develop your piano skills and can apply those new techniques to older repertoire when you return to it.*

≈ *Sometimes it can be difficult to recognize your own improvement because you are practicing each day and the progress is gradual. However, teachers usually hear more improvement because they only check in with their students once or twice a week. Also, teachers are trained to listen for specific technical and musical elements—which is how they judge improvement from one lesson to the next.*

≈ *With respect to using the pedal in a piece, some students find it helpful to include the pedal as they learn the notes of the piece because it helps sustain the sounds as the hands move around. However, others find this too complicated and prefer to learn the notes first and then add the pedal later.*

The Tower Keeper

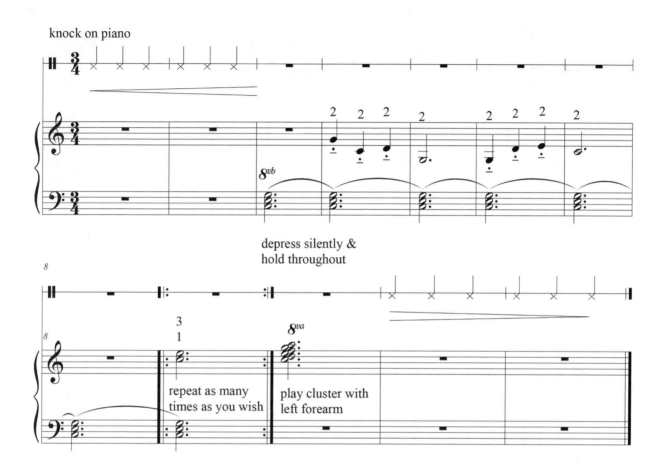

LESSON 34

Chorale-Style Repertoire

This lesson will begin by reviewing the harmonization from the previous lesson that you prepared called "Lavender's Blue"; you will play this with both hands and broken chords in the left hand, comparing your performance to the intructor's. Then, you will be introduced to a new sight-reading example, your goal being to play it to the best of your ability in a short amount of time. Next, you will play through "Ode to Schumann," jumping back in to join the instructor if you make a mistake. You will also learn, measure by measure, a hymnlike piece called a chorale that was written by Robert Schumann; it has mostly the same harmonies as "Ode to Schumann," so your fingers and ears are prepared for this composition. Finally, you will end the lesson by playing "The Tower Keeper" along with the instructor.

There are two famous Schumanns who were pianists and composers. In fact, they were a married couple: Robert (1810–1856) and Clara (1819–1896).

Robert's hopes of having a concert career were dashed when he injured the fourth finger on his right hand (after devising a contraption to strengthen this weak finger). Instead, he turned to composing and writing about music and musicians. He founded the influential journal *Neue Zeitschrift für Musik* and launched the careers of many musicians, including Chopin and Brahms.

Although careers outside of the home were uncommon for women during this time, Clara enjoyed a long performing career. She composed, too; her most well-known composition is a piano trio.

KEY TERMS

CHARACTER PIECES: A group of short pieces for piano, each with a contrasting mood or character.

CHORALE: A style of music that sounds like a hymn; a feature is that the harmony is stacked up in chords, with four parts, and each part (or voice, as it is called) is distributed between the hands.

FERMATA (⌒): Italian word that means "to hold"; colloquially referred to as a pause sign, this symbol indicates that you should hold the note or notes for the full value, plus some extra time (how much time is up to the performer).

PRACTICE ASSIGNMENT

❏ Play the A and G harmonic minor scales and chord progressions.

❏ Play "Ode to Schumann" [p. 126].

❏ Practice sight-reading [p. 133].

❏ Play Schumann's Chorale, op. 68, no. 4 [[p. 133] (first eight measures; hands together; with pedal).

❏ Review any other repertoire that you enjoyed playing previously in the course.

Robert Schumann is best known for his vocal songs with piano accompaniment, a piano concerto, and numerous collections of short piano pieces called character pieces, including *Album for the Young*, a collection of 43 pieces, each with a different style or a unique character and mood.

Clara Schumann edited the first edition of these pieces, so many of the dynamics, fingerings, and musical choices that pianists make when playing these are based on her suggestions.

PRACTICE TIPS

➳ *It is very easy to lose your place visually in a score. If you have to look down at your hands, you'll need to practice looking back up but adjusting your eyes not to where you left off, but ahead in the score (depending on how many beats you played before looking back up). This skill is essential when you are playing with someone else and trying to keep steady.*

➳ *When there are numerous slight shifts in both hands between every measure in a piece, a trick for playing the correct pitches is to try to move or prepare your right hand as the left hand is playing and then to prepare or move the left hand while the right hand is playing. This means that as you are playing and listening to what you are playing, you are already looking ahead in the music and physically preparing your hand.*

➳ *While you might prefer a specific musical style or composer, it is good to play music from different eras when you practice to ensure that you are developing many different types of piano techniques and playing different styles of music.*

➳ *Ideally, you should work on music that is in different stages. In one week, you might work on one brand-new piece, another that you are at the midway point in the learning process, and another that you are in the final stages of perfecting or that you are maintaining.*

➳ *The human brain can hold a very limited amount of new information in working memory (where we process new material), so if you play short sections of a long piece and then repeat these, you can give your brain and fingers time to process the material and learn it more efficiently.*

➳ *In repertoire that becomes familiar and comfortable, eventually you don't have to think as carefully or as consciously about the individual notes. Instead, the score serves as a reference and what you've practiced happens a little more automatically with the fingers. Practicing small sections of tricky material helps you get to this stage sooner when learning piano music.*

Sight-Reading

Spindler
arr. Pike

Chorale, op. 68, no. 4

R. Schumann
arr. Pike

LESSON 35

Impressionism and the Una Corda Pedal

This lesson begins with a warm-up that includes the G harmonic minor scale, the G minor primary chord progression, the A minor primary chord progression, and the A harmonic minor scale. Then, you will be prepared to play the sight-reading example from the previous lesson, which is in A minor and then will be transposed into G minor. Next, you will be introduced to an arrangement in the key of F major called Hungarian Dance no. 6, which is the theme from a much longer work that was written by Johannes Brahms. You will also review Schumann's Chorale, checking in and assessing your progress with the first eight measures and previewing the second half of the piece. Finally, you will learn about impressionistic music. Because so much of this piano music is extremely difficult, you will learn, measure by measure, a short piece called "Gamelan in the Mist," which is within your technical grasp but includes a few elements found in Claude Debussy's music, such as the una corda pedal. Because this piece is in G♭ major, you should play the G♭ major 5-finger pattern before you play it.

As a young composer, the German pianist Johannes Brahms (1833–1897) was championed by Robert Schumann, and even after Robert's death, Clara Schumann regularly performed and advocated for Brahms's music.

A gamelan is an orchestra of traditional Indonesian gongs or bell-type instruments that were of great interest to Debussy and his contemporaries, who were exposed to music and art from the Far East during the Parisian world's fair known as the International Exposition of 1889.

©uskarp/iStock/Thinkstock

THE UNA CORDA PEDAL

The leftmost pedal, called the una corda pedal, is used in a good deal of Claude Debussy's music. It is sometimes called a soft pedal, but that's a misnomer; the pedal actually changes the timbre, or quality of the sound. This was very important in impressionist music.

On a grand piano, when the una corda is depressed, the entire keyboard action shifts to the right. When the hammers strike the strings, they aren't making contact with the well-worn felt (which becomes hard over time), but instead a softer part of the felt plays the string. On some pianos, the difference in sound and tone color, or timbre, is striking.

When the una corda is depressed on an upright piano, the hammers move a little closer to the strings and, thus, there isn't as much velocity with each hammer strike. The tone does tend to get a little softer, but the tone color may change, too.

On a digital piano, depressing the una corda will generally make the sound a little softer. If you have an electronic keyboard that does not have an una corda pedal, just play more softly to produce a different sound effect when called on to play the una corda pedal.

IMPRESSIONISTIC MUSIC

Impressionism is a movement in music that began in France during the late 19th and early 20th centuries. Claude Debussy (1862–1918) was one of the composers who developed a style of musical writing that was what we've come to call impressionistic. He was inspired by impressionist poets, such as Charles Baudelaire, and painters, such as Claude Monet and Pierre-Auguste Renoir.

In experimenting with creating new sounds on the piano, Debussy transformed some key elements in musical composition. He explored how the pedals could be used to change sound and tone color of the instrument. Rather than using harmonies based on 3rds, he was more interested in 4ths, 6ths, 7ths, 9ths and 11ths. In his music, streams of parallel intervals are heard, and dissonances may not be resolved in the traditional way.

Debussy used scales that were considered to be oriental during his day; these are actually traditional modes that are neither major nor minor. He frequently availed of the pentatonic scale, a five-note scale that uses the black keys on the piano. Debussy was a pianist, and he used this instrument to explore this new musical idiom.

Like Bach, he also wrote 24 preludes (Debussy wrote two books of 12 preludes). These are miniature masterpieces, and many of them are written in the impressionistic style. It was especially through his later works that Debussy bridged the Romantic and the 20th-century traditions and paved the way for many innovations of the 20th century that would follow.

Other French composers who wrote piano music in this style include Gabriel Fauré and Maurice Ravel, and some of these pieces are the most difficult in the entire piano repertoire. American composer Charles Griffes also wrote impressionistic piano music.

KEY TERMS

PIANISSIMO: The Italian word indicating to play softer than piano, notated as **_pp_**.

UNA CORDA PEDAL: Sometimes abbreviated as u.c. on the score, it is the left pedal on the piano that changes the timbre, or quality, of the sound; it is depressed with the left foot and held until the end of the piece (if a composer wishes for you to release it sooner, _tre corda_ ("3 strings") will be indicated in the score); you can still pedal normally with the damper or sustain pedal as you hold the una corda ("1 string") pedal.

VIVACE: Italian word that is a tempo marking for a lively speed.

PRACTICE ASSIGNMENT

❑ Play the A, E, and G harmonic minor scales and chord progressions.

❑ Play the G♭ major 5-finger pattern (to prepare for "Gamelan in the Mist").

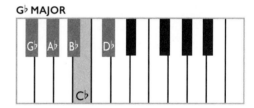

❑ Play the sight-reading from lesson 34 [p. 133] (transpose to G and E minor).

❑ Play Schumann's Chorale [p. 133]. (You can practice "Ode to Schumann" [p. 126] as a warm-up for this piece if that helps you.)

❑ Play Hungarian Dance no. 6 [p. 138] (with hands together for the next lesson, but spend several practice sessions working on the hands separately).

❑ Play "Gamelan in the Mist" [p. 138] (learn it for the next lesson; remember to use the una corda pedal, if you have one, and listen to how this changes the sound on your instrument).

Hungarian Dance no. 6

Brahms
arr. Pike

Gamelan in the Mist

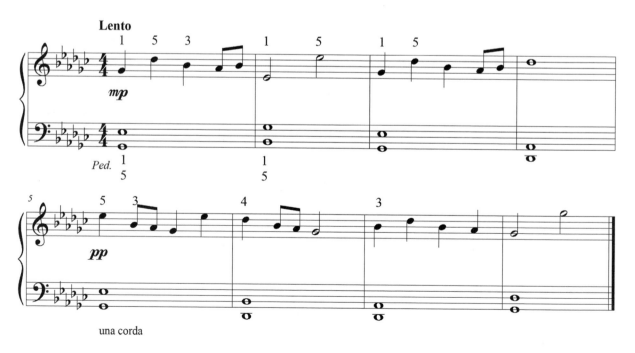

LESSON 36

Triplets and Continuing Piano Study

In this lesson, you will begin by playing the E minor 5-finger pattern with the right hand and the tonic and dominant 7th chord with the left hand. Then, you will be ready to try playing the sight-reading from lesson 34 transposed in the key of E minor. Next, you will play Hungarian Dance no. 6 from the previous lesson. You will also spend some time on "Gamelan in the Mist," eventually playing hands together and with the una corda pedal. Then, you will be introduced to a bonus piece known as Minuet in G Minor, which has been attributed to Johann Sebastian Bach. At this point, you possess all of the skills needed to learn this piece. You will also be introduced to a new rhythmic pattern: eighth-note triplets, which you will learn how to clap and play. Finally, you will learn, measure by measure, how to play the theme from Beethoven's *Moonlight* Sonata.

KEY TERM

EIGHTH-NOTE TRIPLETS: Rhythmic pattern that has three eighth notes joined by a single beam and the number 3, either above or below that beam, depending on the direction of the stems; found in simple meter and have to fit into one quarter-note beat (the same time that you would normally play two eighth notes).

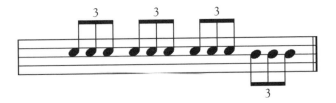

Transposition is a skill that isn't always taught to beginning piano students, especially to adult beginners, but becoming comfortable with many keys and with moving around the keyboard is an important part of gaining the confidence necessary to play the challenging pieces that are part of the piano literature.

PRACTICE ASSIGNMENT

- ❑ Play the E minor 5-finger pattern.

- ❑ Play the triplet exercises for this lesson [below].

- ❑ Play Hungarian Dance no. 6 [p. 138].

- ❑ Play "Gamelan in the Mist" [p. 138].

- ❑ Play Minuet in G Minor [p. 141].

- ❑ Play the theme from Beethoven's *Moonlight* Sonata [p. 142].

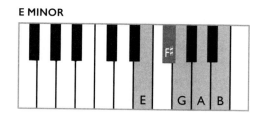

Triplet Exercises

EXERCISE 1

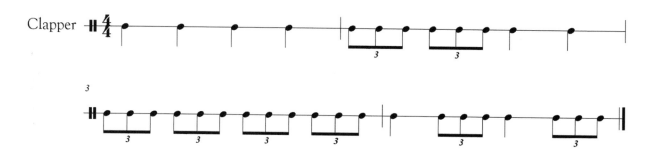

EXERCISE 2

Minuet in G Minor BWV Anh 115 (abridged)

J. S. Bach
arr. Pike

Theme from *Moonlight* Sonata

Beethoven
arr. Pike

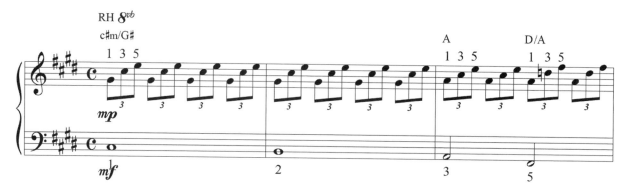

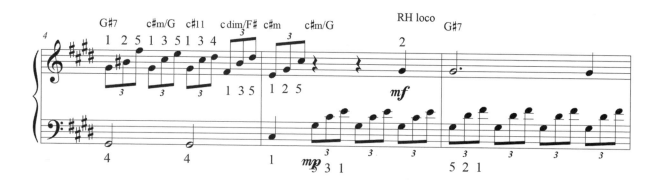

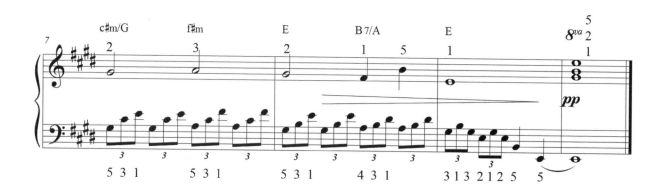

NOTES FOR FURTHER PIANO STUDY

After completing this course, you may be satisfied with your newfound knowledge and feel that you can continue to explore new repertoire and develop your piano skills on your own. However, you may wish to dive more deeply into specific technique or music or fill in some gaps that have inevitably arisen during this course.

If this is the case, you may wish to pursue piano study with a teacher, either online or in person. At this point, you may find that having face-to-face (in-person) or synchronous online lessons to be helpful as you'll get immediate feedback from a teacher. Piano lessons can take place either in a group setting (where there are multiple keyboards in the classroom and you'll work with the instructor over headphones individually and out loud with the group) or individually with an instructor. There are benefits to each type of lesson, so explore the options for either group or private study in your community.

However, it is recommended that you find a qualified, professional piano teacher who specializes in working with adults. You can find a qualified professional by visiting the Music Teachers National Association website at mtna.org. This is the largest professional association for music teachers in North America, and there is a find-a-teacher function on the website. Some teachers become a Nationally Certified Teacher of Music (NCTM); this designation demonstrates a commitment to teaching. You should also inquire about which degrees your teacher has earned. Some pianists specialize in piano pedagogy, which means that they have had rigorous courses in teaching and been provided with feedback on their teaching from qualified faculty members.

Before registering for lessons, ask about an interview. Professional teachers will want an opportunity to meet you, to learn about your goals and objectives for music study, and to share their teaching philosophy with you. Both you and your potential teacher need to know if you'll work well together before making a long-term commitment to lessons. Before the interview, prepare several pieces of music to play and write down your goals for music lessons—being as specific as you can be—so that you can clearly articulate these during the interview. A good piano teacher will help facilitate your learning objectives and goals by providing a curriculum that will help you continue developing your piano technique and skills.

Composers and Features of Time Periods in Music History

Performance practice was different for each of the time periods in music history. There is some blurriness with the beginnings and endings of time periods, but for the purposes of this course, think of the baroque period as lasting from 1600–1750; the classical period from about 1725–1800; the Romantic era from about 1800–1910; and the contemporary or modern period from 1910 onward.

BAROQUE PERIOD

It is in the baroque period of music history that the first standard keyboard music appears. Important baroque composers include Johann Sebastian Bach, George Frideric Handel, Claudio Monteverdi (who was influential in the development of opera during this period), Jean-Baptiste Lully (who influenced violin and orchestral technique), Johann Pachelbel, Antonio Vivaldi, Jean-Philippe Rameau, and Henry Purcell. Other important keyboard composers include Georg Philipp Telemann and Domenico Scarlatti.

Johann Sebastian Bach and George Frideric Handel were both born in 1685 and died at the close of the baroque era within nine years of each other.

While there are distinct styles within the baroque era, in general the style of artwork, architecture, and music became quite florid and extravagant during this period. Music of the baroque era is known for its unflagging rhythmic drive (seemingly never resting until the end of a piece), melodies that were often florid and embellished, and music that was contrapuntal (which uses counterpoint, the practice of playing two or more melodic lines simultaneously, rather than having a single melody accompanied by chords).

The overall effect of baroque music is that it sounds complex and is full of emotion; keyboard works, in particular, could be showy or improvisational. During this time, fewer church modes (which were other kinds of scales used in religious music) were used, and the major and minor tonality became the primary modes used by composers.

Common types or forms of baroque keyboard music included dance suites (multimovement works that contained stylized dances), preludes and fugues, toccatas, fantasias, and sonatas. Note, however, that sonatas in the baroque era were not the same as those in subsequent periods. Scarlatti wrote more than 500 sonatas for the piano; these are primarily one-movement works and are in binary, or two-part, form. The sonata-allegro form had not developed yet.

One playing innovation, for which Scarlatti receives credit, is the use of frequent hand crossing in his sonatas. Like much of the keyboard music of the time, performers were expected to embellish the melody with trills, mordents, and the like. Indeed, a shorthand was developed for notating these in the score; thus, they were not written out. It is still common practice today to simply notate the symbol for the embellishments above the melody line, and performers are expected to know how to realize or play them. While there are several good books and editions of music that illustrate how each embellishment is meant to be played, the primary source material comes from Carl Philipp Emanuel Bach's important treatise, "Essay on the True Art of Playing Keyboard Instruments," which was published in two parts, in 1753 and 1762.

Another common form of the multimovement sonata during this time was called a trio sonata, in which there were three different staves of music on the written scores. But although it sounds like there would be three players, such sonatas actually required four performers. There were usually two unspecified solo instruments (for example, a violin or flute); a bass player (performing on the precursor to the modern-day cello); and a keyboardist, who realized or improvised an accompaniment based on the figured bass (as the Roman numerals and figures were included below the staves).

CLASSICAL PERIOD

The classical period is when the piano as we know it came into being. Prior to that time, harpsichords, organs, and clavichords were the main keyboard instruments. And while they share characteristics with the modern piano, the action was quite different.

The forms of the classical era are less complex, in many ways, than those in the baroque era, and there is more piano music that is accessible to you as a beginning pianist from this time. That doesn't mean that the music is easy, especially the more advanced literature. While some of the music from the classical era sounds simple and easy, it's actually extremely difficult, requiring great technical finesse.

Composers from the classical period include three of Johann Sebastian Bach's sons: Carl Philipp Emanuel Bach (who worked for Frederick the Great in Berlin and Potsdam); Johann Christian Bach (known as the London Bach because he made his career

Johann Christian Bach influenced a very young Mozart when he traveled to London.

there); and Wilhelm Friedemann Bach. Other important composers include Franz Joseph Haydn, Wolfgang Amadeus Mozart, and Ludwig van Beethoven (though Beethoven straddled both the classical and Romantic eras).

Some features of music in the classical period are clarity, balance, and emotional restraint, especially when compared with other time periods. This was the period of the Enlightenment, when there was a shift away from the dominance of the church toward freedom of thought and empirical study. That's why it's sometimes called the age of reason. During the classical period, the aristocracy became very influential in supporting the arts. This was especially true in Germany and Austria, where aristocrats served as patrons to composers and artists. Because music was needed for social and other occasions within the court, composers and performers were charged with producing excellent music for a class of people with very sophisticated tastes. It was also during this era that many public concert halls and theaters were built, which created increased demand for music. The piano became a household instrument during this time, and publishing houses began printing music (but piano scores, in particular, became widely available). As more amateur players began reading musical notation, sometimes detailed articulation, which was typical performance practice at the time, was included in the score.

As the classical period progressed, new musical forms were developed and popularized. Common types of music from the classical period include the symphony, various forms of chamber music, concertos (that feature the orchestra and a solo instrument), and opera (which became very popular among both aristocratic audiences and the bourgeoisie). Instrumental music often took the form of the sonata, a specific kind of multimovement work that usually consists of three or four movements.

ROMANTIC PERIOD

The French Revolution ushered in the new age known as the Romantic period, but it was musicians in Germany and Austria who played an important role in the development of a Romantic musical style. Artists who emerged as influential early on in the Romantic era were concerned with individual expression and breaking free of what they saw as the constraints of classical form and limited harmony.

The Industrial Revolution caused a shift in the economic status for many people in Europe. This meant that composers could no longer rely on patrons to sustain their work. But more people could avail of music, either by listening to it in the concert hall or by playing it at home. However, music became much more technically demanding during the Romantic era, so while music-publishing and piano-making businesses were plentiful, the new music was much too difficult for the average person. Thus, conservatories, where music was taught and artists were trained, became important establishments during the Romantic era.

Virtuosic performers were all the rage in the 19th century (think Franz Liszt on the piano and Niccolò Paganini on the violin), but outstanding teachers—such as Robert Schumann, Felix Mendelssohn, and Liszt—also gained great fame. The field of music criticism was born during the Romantic era. Both Liszt and Schumann wrote excellent articles that were literary masterpieces, and they were influential critics of their day. It was also during this time that researchers began to rediscover and print complete collections of master composers, such as Bach, Mozart, and Beethoven.

Due to the individual nature of artists and composers, it's very difficult to define a Romantic style. Art songs (for voice and piano), opera, ballet, symphonies, and instrumental forms (such as variations, rhapsodies, and études) were popular. The sonata was still an important form for instrumental music, but it became longer and much more complex. Now, for example, instead of just two themes, an exposition might have three or more. And the harmonies used became complicated, and modulations moved farther away from the home key. While there was still a tonal center in Romantic music, as the 19th century wore on, tonality was gradually eroded.

Melodies and rhythms became more intense and complex, and music had a thicker texture— meaning that there could be many more layers of sound, even in a solo piano work. There might be a soaring melody while rhapsodic arpeggios across the keyboard filled in the harmony. Use of the pedal required more refinement. The technical demands of compositions increased, and individual instrumental technique improved, especially among pianists.

It was also during the Romantic era that improvisation became less important. Master musicians and performers still learned and practiced this skill, but few improvised in the concert hall before live audiences. In fact, even the cadenzas—the flashy solo passages in concerti that had previously been improvised only (Mozart never supplied a written-out cadenza)—were now notated in the score.

There are far too many composers to mention, but in the piano world, important composers from the Romantic era include Ludwig van Beethoven, Franz Schubert, Frédéric Chopin, Robert Schumann, Franz Liszt, and Johannes Brahms.

During the Romantic era, concert pianists and the piano developed simultaneously and forever changed the piano repertoire. Beethoven, who straddled both classical and Romantic periods, was notorious for breaking strings on his pianos and favoring more heavily weighted keyboards. This may have been due in part to his failing hearing, but he was pushing the boundaries of piano technique and musical harmony at the end of his life. He eagerly tried out new instruments, with longer keyboards and innovative mechanical systems, as piano makers created them. In fact, we can even trace the development of the piano through his sonatas.

But the real change for pianos came about during the Industrial Revolution, and it was the introduction of the cast-iron frame that allowed pianos to become bigger, heavier, and sturdier and hold much more tension in the strings. This was the advent of the modern piano. Such a piano could project even the softest notes to the back row of a large concert hall. But because of the heavier action, it required a new kind of piano technique. There were different camps of piano technique throughout Europe in this time period, and piano technique improved vastly and became codified, passed from one generation to the next through master teachers and their apprentices.

Virtuosic performers, such as Liszt, played with a free, relaxed technique, but there was also power, arm weight, and more movement of the hands and arm than in previous generations. Liszt took what he learned from formal studies with pianists and their pupils, such as Carl Czerny (a student of Beethoven), and informal meetings with others, such as Frédéric Chopin, and brought it to the next level, changing piano technique forever.

MODERN PERIOD

Modern classical music tends to be quite original and diverse, and it can be filled with new and interesting ways to produce sound on traditional instruments and through technology. At the end of the 19th century and early in the 20th century, some composers wrote programmatic music, where a picture or story was conveyed through the instrumental composition. As the 20th century progressed, there was a trend toward nationalism by some composers. Many incorporated folk songs into their music or wrote melodies that evoked folk tunes from particular cultures. Such composers included Ralph Vaughan Williams in England, Jean Sibelius in Finland, Béla Bartók in Hungary, Leoš Janáček in Czechoslovakia, and any number of Russian composers.

In general, in the 20th century, melodies became less lyrical and included more wide leaps and disjunct movements. They might also be made up of short, melodic motives or fragments. Rhythms might be asymmetric, and meter might even change multiple times within a composition. Sometimes composers wrote polyrhythms (where different rhythmic patterns were played simultaneously). Harmony also changed, becoming much more dissonant. Among some composers there was a complete breakdown of tonality, such than one cannot tell whether a piece is in a major or minor mode, or a piece could have been in multiple tonalities at once. Some music was even atonal.

Composers such as Arnold Schoenberg employed the 12-tone technique of writing music, where all 12 pitches in an octave were assigned a number, called a tone row, and each had to be used before the composer could reuse a pitch. Some music was aleatory, or left some elements to chance; there might be instructions for the performer to choose a unique rhythm or set of pitches that could be played in any order or improvised during performance.

In the 1960s, American and French composers began experimenting with using computer-generated music, sounds, or recorded music alongside live performances. And composers explored alternate means to producing sound on traditional instruments. On the piano, these are called extended piano techniques. A performer might be instructed to reach inside the piano and pluck strings or play tone clusters on the keyboard with the forearm.

Some composers even wrote music for the so-called prepared piano. To prepare a piano, one must follow a detailed list of instructions, which usually includes placing all kinds of objects—such as paper, erasers, and paper clips—between the strings of a grand piano so that when the hammer strikes each string, a very unique sound is produced.

While there is a good deal of more traditional sounding classical music that comes from the modern era, many avant-garde composers were pushing the boundaries of music harmony, melody, tonality, and other features that had been in place for generations.

The Development of the Piano

Bartolomeo Cristofori (1655–1731) from Florence is credited with inventing the first piano sometime before 1709. He called it the *gravicembalo col piano e forte*, which might loosely translate into "harpsichord that plays piano and forte." The instrument itself was much smaller and produced a noticeably different tone than the modern piano, but it also produced a very different tone from the harpsichord or clavichord, which preceded it. Throughout the classical period, this instrument came to be called the fortepiano (which is opposite to how we name the instrument today). These keyboards were not as long as the modern piano and had only 4 to 4½ octaves.

The inner action of Cristofori's piano resembled the modern piano, but the case looked like a harpsichord. The harpsichord's sound was created through plectra plucking the stings. Now, however, little hammers struck the strings, and a more complicated action (which Cristofori patented in 1709) was employed. This meant that the pianist's arm weight affected tone and dynamics. Unlike the modern piano, in which the hammers are made of felt, the hammer heads on the early pianos were covered with leather.

There were two other innovations in Cristofori's instrument: the escapement action (which permits the hammer to fall back from the string while the key is still depressed) and the check of the hammer's return (which allows for faster repetition of notes).

Although the first piano was created in Italy, news of the instrument spread. Germany had several notable fortepiano innovators. Gottfried Silbermann (1683–1753), a clavichord and organ maker in Dresden, continued to hone the escapement and action of the instrument.

Johann Sebastian Bach played one of Silbermann's earliest pianos, and though he appreciated the dynamic possibilities, Bach complained about the weakness of the tone in the higher register and about the heavy action—the keys were much more difficult to depress than a harpsichord or clavichord. However, sometime later, his reaction to playing a newer Silbermann piano was more positive.

In a letter written on October 17 and 18 in 1777, Mozart told of how Stein ensured that his pianos would hold up to common household wear and tear. If Mozart is to be believed, Stein put his piano out in sun and snow, and even made cracks and glued them back together, to ensure that his instruments were sturdy and would still play well. In the same letter, Mozart wrote about the responsiveness of the knee-lever innovation; the first pedals on fortepianos were on the underside of the instrument cabinet and controlled by the knee.

Johann Andreas Stein (1728–1792) innovated by using a separate escapement action for each individual key, rather than one wooden rod, called a rail, for all of the keys. Mozart liked Stein pianos. Another of Mozart's favored pianos was made by a Viennese piano maker named Anton Walter (1752–1826).

By the end of the 18th century, there were also piano makers in other countries. Sébastian Érard (1752–1831) in Paris was favored by many musicians of the day (including Haydn), as his fortepianos had a lighter action than the German instruments. In London, a German immigrant, Johann Zumpe, was producing pianos that Johann Christian Bach played. John Broadwood also became an important piano maker in London during this time.

By the end of the 18th century, fortepianos were either square (like the clavichord) or more harpsichord-shaped (resembling the modern grand piano), much as today there are uprights and grands.

One of the pianos that Anton Walter made for Mozart can still be seen at the Mozart museum in Salzburg, Austria. The colors of the keys are opposite to current piano keys (this is how harpsichord keys looked at the time), so the white keys were the groups of twos and threes on the keyboard. This piano had a five-octave range and leather hammers. It also had two knee levers: one to dampen the sound and the other to create muting effects. This fortepiano was considerably bigger and heavier than a harpsichord; it weighed 140 pounds. Of course, by comparison, a modern concert grand weighs about 1000 pounds.

Glossary

Use the diagram below to help identify the musical terms and notation defined in this book.

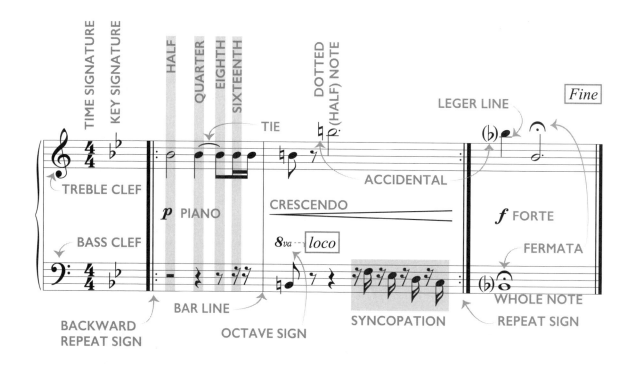

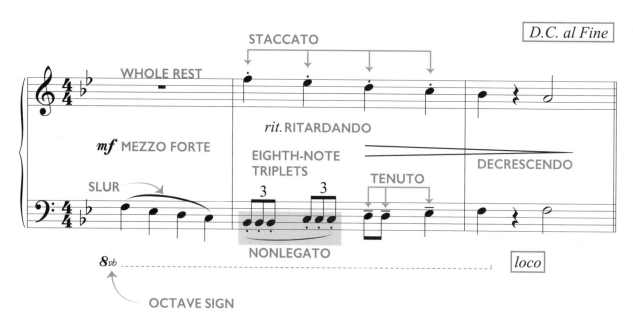

7TH CHORD: A four-note chord consisting of a triad and a 7th interval. [LESSON 24]

12-BAR BLUES: A chord progression that has three four-bar phrases and is one of the typical blues progressions. [LESSON 9]

12-TONE TECHNIQUE: Technique of writing music in which all 12 pitches in an octave are assigned a number (called a tone row) and each has to be used before the composer can reuse a pitch. [LESSON 33]

ACCIDENTAL: A sign—such as a sharp, flat, or natural sign—that is placed in front of a note on the staff to indicate a change in pitch. [LESSON 6]

ALEATORY: Music that leaves some elements to chance (i.e., there might be instructions for the performer to choose a unique rhythm, or set of pitches, which could be played in any order or improvised during performance). [LESSON 33]

ALLEGRO: Italian word that is a tempo marking for a fast, lively speed. [LESSON 16]

ANACRUSIS: A pickup note. [LESSON 16]

ANDANTE: Italian word that is a tempo marking for a walking pace. [LESSON 16]

ARPEGGIO: A broken chord. [LESSON 9]

ARTICULATION: In music, the quality of whether notes are connected to each other or detached. [LESSON 14]

ATONAL: Music that avoids musical tonality. [LESSON 33]

BACKWARD REPEAT SIGN: Indicates that at some point subsequently you'll see a repeat sign, but instead of going all the way back to the beginning of the score, you'll repeat the segment of music from this sign (notated as ‖:). [LESSON 12]

BAR LINE: The vertical line that divides the notes into equal numbers of beats. [LESSON 2]

BASS: Lower notes or sounds; notated on a bass staff and indicated with a bass clef (𝄢). [LESSON 4]

BLOCKED: Form of playing chords in which all notes are played at once. [LESSON 5]

BLOCKING: A practice technique that can be applied to any piece that contains chord patterns and involves playing each complete chord on the downbeat. [LESSON 11]

BROKEN: Form of playing chords in which the pianist plays the bottom note, middle note, top note, and then back down. [LESSON 5]

CADENCE: A chord sequence that resolves at the end of a piece or phrase and that should sound and feel like a resting place. [LESSON 7]

CANTABILE: Italian word that musicians translate as "in a singing style"; it means to listen to your playing, try to shape your phrases, and (often) play legato. [LESSON 22]

CHARACTER PIECES: A group of short pieces for piano, each with a contrasting mood or character. [LESSON 34]

CHORALE: A style of music that sounds like a hymn; a feature is that the harmony is stacked up in chords, with four parts, and each part (or voice, as it is called) is distributed between the hands. [LESSON 34]

CHORD: Three or more notes played together; often used to create harmony. [LESSON 5]

CHORD TONES: The notes contained in each chord. [LESSON 7]

COMMON TIME: See **QUADRUPLE METER**; sometimes represented by a " **C** " at the beginning of a piece instead of $\frac{4}{4}$. [LESSON 19]

COMPOUND METER: A class of meters in which each beat is subdivided into three sub-beats; typically has an 8 on the bottom of the time signature, which tells the kind of note that serves as the sub-beat, while the top number is usually 3, 6, or 9. [LESSON 19]

CONTRAPUNTAL MUSIC: Music that uses counterpoint. [LESSON 30]

COUNTERPOINT: The practice of playing two or more melodic lines simultaneously, rather than having a single melody accompanied by chords. [LESSON 30]

CRESCENDO: To gradually get louder or stronger, abbreviated cres. (or cresc.) or represented as a long less-than sign in mathematics. [LESSON 15]

D.C. AL FINE: An indication to go back to the head—D.C. stands for da capo, which means "the head"—of the piece (the top of the piece, or the beginning) and play until you see the "fine" sign. [LESSON 31]

DA CAPO: Italian phrase that means "the head." [LESSON 31]

DAMPER PEDAL: The pedal on the far right of your piano—regardless of how many pedals your piano has—that you depress with your right foot to lift the dampers (which contain the felt that dampens the strings, or stops them from vibrating), causing all of the strings to ring until you release the pedal. [LESSON 12]

DECRESCENDO: See **DIMINUENDO**. [LESSON 15]

DELIBERATE PRACTICE: Also called self-regulation, practice that involves three steps: forethought, volitional control, and self-evaluation/reflection. [LESSON 32]

DEVELOPMENT: The second section in sonata form, in which the composer develops one or more of the themes from the exposition. [LESSON 24]

DIMINUENDO: To gradually get softer, abbreviated dim. or represented as a long greater-than sign in mathematics. [LESSON 15]

DOMINANT: The fifth scale degree. [LESSON 3]

DOMINANT CHORD: The chord that is built on the fifth scale degree. [LESSON 7]

DOTTED NOTE: A note head with a dot placed after it that adds half of the value of the regular note. [LESSON 1]

DOTTED RHYTHMS: A rhythm with uneven or slightly unsteady notes. [LESSON 16]

DOUBLE FLAT (♭♭): A whole step below the original note; represented by two flat signs. [LESSON 24]

DOUBLE SHARP (×): A whole step above the original note. [LESSON 24]

DUPLE METER: A meter that has two beats per measure, and each beat is a quarter-note long; represented as $\frac{2}{4}$. [LESSON 19]

DYNAMICS: In music, changes in the intensity of the sound. [LESSON 3]

EIGHTH NOTE: Rhythmic symbol that has a solid black head and a straight stem with one flag; held for half of a count, or beat. [LESSON 18]

EIGHTH-NOTE TRIPLETS: Rhythmic pattern that has three eighth notes joined by a single beam and the number 3, either above or below that beam, depending on the direction of the stems; found in simple meter and have to fit into one quarter-note beat (the same time that you would normally play two eighth notes). [LESSON 36]

ENHARMONIC: Relating to notes that sound like the same pitch and look like the same key on the piano but are written differently on the staff. [LESSON 6]

ÉTUDE: From the French word that means "study," a piece of music focused on a specific skill that is developed with practice. [LESSON 2]

EXPOSITION: The first section in sonata form, in which the themes are introduced. [LESSON 24]

FERMATA (⌢): Italian word that means "to hold"; colloquially referred to as a pause sign, this symbol indicates that you should hold the note or notes for the full value, plus some extra time (how much time is up to the performer). [LESSON 34]

FIGURED BASS: A bass line that has the harmonies shown by numbers, or figures, rather than written out as chords. [LESSON 9]

FINE: Italian word that means "finish" or "ending." [LESSON 31]

FLAT (♭): The symbol used in music to indicate that a note or pitch should be lowered by a half step; when a flat is placed in front of a note, that note remains flat for the entire measure, unless otherwise indicated. [LESSON 6]

FORTE: The Italian term for "loud" or "strong," notated as $\boldsymbol{f}$. [LESSON 3]

FUGUE: A contrapuntal piece in which there is a theme called a subject—which is introduced in several voices, both at the original pitch and in transposed versions—as well as a theme known as the answer to the subject. [LESSON 31]

GROUND BASS: A bass line that is repeated over and over throughout a piece. [LESSON 31]

HALF NOTE: Rhythmic symbol that has an open head and a stem; held for two counts, or beats. [LESSON 1]

HARMONIC INTERVAL: A type of interval in which the notes are played simultaneously. [LESSON 6]

HARMONIC MINOR: The form of the minor scale in which the seventh scale degree is raised by half a step on the way up and on the way down. [LESSON 21]

HARMONY: Pitches that are played simultaneously, such as chords. [LESSON 3]

INTERVAL: The distance between two notes. [LESSON 4]

INTERVALLIC READING: Reading by referencing specific landmark notes and then using the intervals to figure out the subsequent notes. [LESSON 4]

INVERSIONS: The different positions that chords can be put in when altering the way the notes on the staff are stacked up for each chord. [LESSON 9]

KEY SIGNATURE: Indicates the sharps or flats in any given key and is found at the beginning of the staff, immediately following the treble or bass clef; the order of the sharps and flats in the key signature is always the same. [LESSON 9]

LANDMARK NOTES: Notes whose location on the keyboard are learned well that help the player figure out other notes' locations. [LESSON 4]

LEAD LINE: A melody that is presented with the chord symbols above it instead of having Roman numerals; common in piano and vocal scores, particularly in books that have Broadway tunes. [LESSON 13]

LEGATO: The Italian term for "tied together," a type of articulation where the notes are connected and played smoothly; notated with a slur (curved line). [LESSON 14]

LEGER LINE: A snippet of a line that is added above or below a musical staff to lengthen its range. [LESSON 5]

LH: Left hand. [LESSON 1]

LOCO: Italian word meaning to play as written; indication often seen following a passage where your hand has been displaced by an octave as a reminder to no longer play at that octave and to resume playing as written on the staff. [LESSON 29]

MAJOR: Describes the type of mode being played in; one of the two most commonly encountered modes in Western classical music; sounds lighter than the minor mode. [LESSON 2]

MEASURE: The space between each bar line. [LESSON 2]

MELODIC INTERVAL: A type of interval in which the notes are played in sequence, one after the other. [LESSON 6]

MELODIC MINOR: The form of the minor scale in which both the sixth and seventh scale degrees are raised by a half step on the ascent but are lowered on the descent. [LESSON 21]

MELODY: The tune of a piece or single pitches, played one after another. [LESSON 3]

METER: The property of music that is based on an underlying, repeating beat rhythm. [LESSON 2]

METRONOME: A simple device that you can program to click at a particular tempo, measured in beats per minute (bpm). [LESSON 4]

MEZZO FORTE: The Italian term for "moderately loud," notated as ***mf***. [LESSON 11]

MINOR: Describes the type of mode being played in; one of the two most commonly encountered modes in Western classical music; sounds darker than the major mode. [LESSON 13]

MODALITY: Playing in a given mode, such as major or minor. [LESSON 13]

MODERATO: Italian word that is a tempo marking for a moderate speed. [LESSON 16]

MODULATION: The act of moving from one key and firmly establishing a new key within a piece. [LESSON 24]

NATURAL MINOR: The form of the minor scale that occurs when we start on the tonic and, moving up by step, play only the notes in the key signature. [LESSON 21]

NATURAL SIGN (♮): A sign indicating that a note should return to its normal, or natural, pitch; just like the other accidentals (flat and sharp), the natural sign is placed before the pitch and on the same line or in the same space as the note being altered and lasts for the remainder of the measure. [LESSON 6]

NONCHORD TONES: Notes that are not chord tones. [LESSON 7]

NONLEGATO: An articulation that indicates to play the notes somewhat detached from one to the next. [LESSON 14]

NOTE HEAD: The round part of a rhythmic symbol that provides important information about its note name or pitch, which corresponds with a specific piano key. [LESSON 1]

OCTAVE SIGN: A sign placed above the staff to mean play one octave higher (***8va***) or placed below the staff to mean play one octave lower (***8vb***). [LESSON 14]

PARALLEL KEYS: Keys whose key signatures are different but that share the same letter name (i.e., D major and D minor). [LESSON 20]

PASSING TONE: A nonchord tone that moves by step from one note of a chord to the next. [LESSON 17]

PEDAL TONE: A single bass note from the harmony that is held through numerous measures, even when that note isn't part of the chord. [LESSON 25]

PIANISSIMO: The Italian word indicating to play softer than piano, notated as **_pp_**. [LESSON 35]

PIANO: The Italian word for "soft," notated as **_p_**. [LESSON 3]

PICARDY THIRD: A major third in the final chord that ends a minor composition, rather than a minor 3rd; a very common technique in music. [LESSON 22]

PITCH: The specific note that is played on the piano. [LESSON 1]

POLYRHYTHM: Rhythm that contains different rhythmic patterns played simultaneously. [LESSON 33]

PRIMARY CHORD PROGRESSION: A tonic-subdominant-dominant-tonic progression that is the most basic chord progression at the heart of Western music. [LESSON 7]

PRIMARY CHORDS: The three most commonly used chords in any key; the tonic (first scale degree), subdominant (fourth scale degree), and dominant (fifth scale degree) tones of the scale. [LESSON 7]

PROGRAMMATIC MUSIC: Type of music in which a picture or story is conveyed through the instrumental composition. [LESSON 33]

QUADRUPLE METER: A meter that has four beats per measure, and each beat is a quarter-note long; represented as $\frac{4}{4}$. [LESSON 19]

QUARTER NOTE: Rhythmic symbol that has a solid black head and a stem; held for one count, or beat. [LESSON 1]

RECAPITULATION: The third section in sonata form, in which the exposition is recapped. [LESSON 24]

RELATIVE MINOR: Major and minor scales that have the same key signature. [LESSON 15]

REPEAT SIGN: A symbol placed on the score to indicate a repeat (:‖). [LESSON 3]

RESOLUTION: The quality that certain chords have when they lead toward or have a tendency to go toward certain other chords, resulting in a very satisfying sound. [LESSON 7]

REST: Silence in music. [LESSON 1]

RH: Right hand. [LESSON 1]

RHYTHM: How music is organized in time. [LESSON 1]

RITARDANDO: Italian word indicating to become gradually slower, abbreviated rit. [LESSON 28]

RONDEAU: A French musical and poetic form from the 14th and 15th centuries; also popular in French harpsichord music of the baroque era; features a refrain that returns between subsidiary sections. [LESSON 31]

RONDO: A musical form with five or more sections featuring a recurring main section (i.e., ABACA). [LESSON 31]

ROOT POSITION: When the name of the chord, or root, is the bottom note. [LESSON 9]

ROOT: The chord's name or which scale degree it's built upon. [LESSON 9]

RUBATO: Italian word meaning "to steal" or "to rob time"; the practice of pushing forward with the tempo and lingering slightly before regaining some speed without changing the basic pulse; common during the Romantic era. [LESSON 28]

SCALE: A group of notes that often move in a stepwise motion. [LESSON 2]

SECONDARY CHORDS: The four chords that are not primary chords but must go to a primary chord for resolution; the second, third, sixth, and seventh tones of the scale. [LESSON 17]

SEQUENCE: Repeating patterns starting on different pitches. [LESSON 11]

SHADOWING: A practice step that involves placing your hand over the keys that you will use in a piece and then tapping the keys, without depressing them, and saying the note names. [LESSON 2]

SHARP (♯): The symbol used in music to indicate that a note or pitch should be raised by a half step; when a sharp is placed in front of a note, that note remains sharp for the entire measure, unless otherwise indicated. [LESSON 6]

SIGHT-READING: The practice of trying to play a piece of music as well as you can on the first try. [LESSON 11]

SIMPLE METER: A class of meters in which each beat is subdivided into two sub-beats. [LESSON 19]

SIXTEENTH NOTE: Rhythmic symbol that has a solid black head and a straight stem with two flags; held for a quarter of a count, or beat. [LESSON 18]

SLUR: A curved line that connects notes of different pitches that should be played smoothly (legato). [LESSON 5]

SONATA: A multimovement work (usually consisting of three or four movements). [LESSON 24]

SONATINA: A short sonata. [LESSON 24]

STACCATO: The Italian term for "detached" or "disconnected," a type of articulation where the notes are short, or crisp and detached; played even shorter than nonlegato; notated with a dot above or below the notehead (♩). [LESSON 14]

STAFF: The lines and spaces on which notes and pitches are notated. A staff has five lines and four spaces, and each of these is numbered from bottom to top. [LESSON 2]

SUBDOMINANT CHORD: The chord that is built on the fourth scale degree. [LESSON 7]

SUBITO: Italian word that means "suddenly." [LESSON 22]

SUSPENSION: The creation of dissonance by prolonging a note (often across a bar line) that is part of the harmony from the previous measure while the new harmony begins; the dissonance is resolved by moving the dissonant note down by a step. [LESSON 22]

SYNCOPATION: The action of playing or clapping on weaker beats and holding the note through the stronger beats. [LESSON 21]

TEMPO: How fast or slow music is being played. [LESSON 4]

TENUTO: Italian word meaning "to hold"; the mark indicates to hold the note for its full value or can be a weak accent mark; notated with a line above or below the notehead (♩). [LESSON 23]

TETRACHORD PATTERNS: A series of four notes with a specific pattern of whole steps and half steps. [LESSON 15]

TIE: A curved line that connects notes of the same pitch across a bar line. [LESSON 5]

TIME SIGNATURE: The numerical representation at the beginning of a piece used to identify and describe the meter of the piece. [LESSON 2]

TONIC: The first note of the scale being played. Because each note is called a scale degree, most often the tonic is the first scale degree. [LESSON 3]

TONIC CHORD: The chord that is built on the first scale degree. [LESSON 7]

TRANSPOSE: To transfer a melody into another key so that it begins on a different note or pitch. [LESSON 4]

TREBLE: Higher notes or sounds; notated on a treble staff and indicated with a treble clef (𝄞). [LESSON 4]

TRIAD: A three-note chord consisting of a root note and 3rd and 5th intervals. [LESSON 5]

TRIO SONATA: A form of the multimovement sonata that has three different staves of music on the written scores, but—although it sounds like there would be three players—such sonatas actually required four performers (usually two unspecified solo instruments, a bass player, and a keyboardist who realized or improvised an accompaniment based on the figured bass). [LESSON 30]

TRIPLE METER: A meter that has three beats per measure, and each beat is a quarter-note long; represented as $\frac{3}{4}$. [LESSON 19]

UNA CORDA PEDAL: Sometimes abbreviated as u.c. on the score, it is the left pedal on the piano that changes the timbre, or quality, of the sound; it is depressed with the left foot and held until the end of the piece (if a composer wishes for you to release it sooner, *tre corda* ("3 strings") will be indicated in the score); you can still pedal normally with the damper or sustain pedal as you hold the una corda ("1 string") pedal. [LESSON 35]

VIVACE: Italian word that is a tempo marking for a lively speed. [LESSON 35]

WHOLE NOTE: Rhythmic symbol that has an open head with no stem; held for four counts, or beats. [LESSON 1]

Circle of Fifths

The circle of fifths is a tool to help visualize the relationship between keys, which aids in composition, harmonization, and transposition. Traveling clockwise from the top, each pitch is a fifth above the previous pitch.

MAJOR

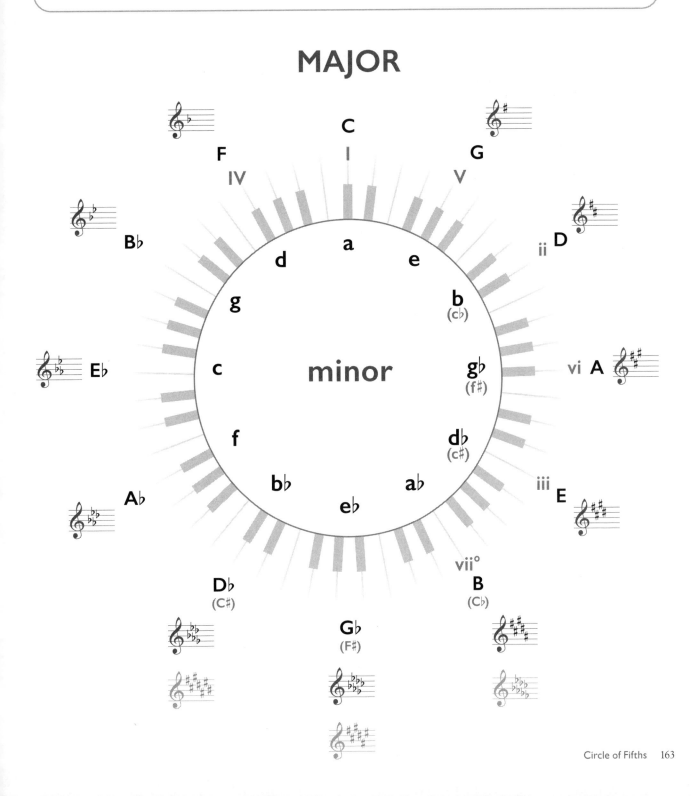

Major 5-Finger Patterns and Primary Chord Progressions

All patterns, chord progressions, scales, and arpeggios follow the circle of fifths [p. 163].

C MAJOR

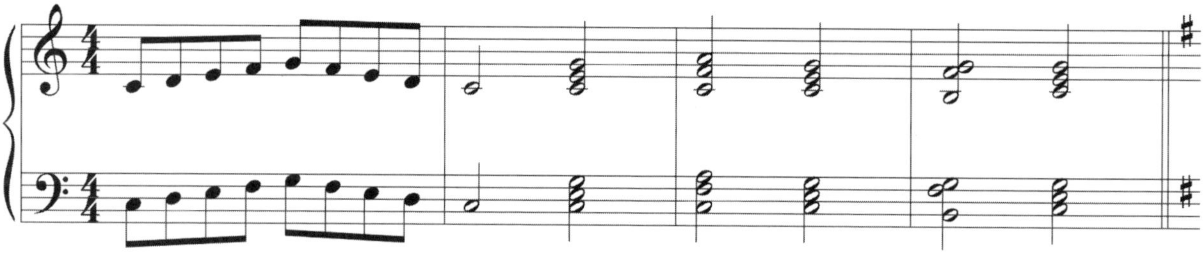

G MAJOR

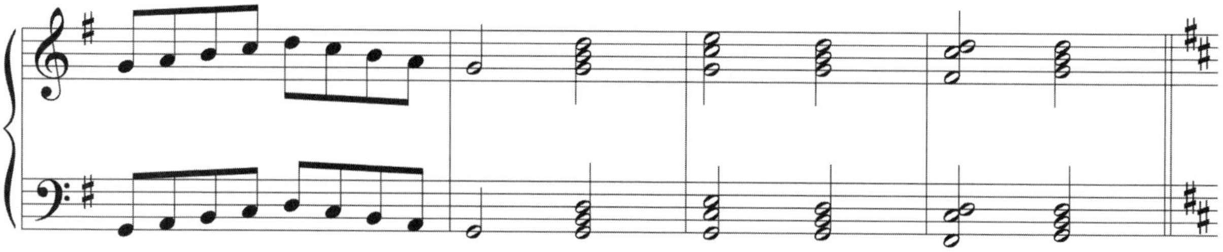

D MAJOR

A MAJOR

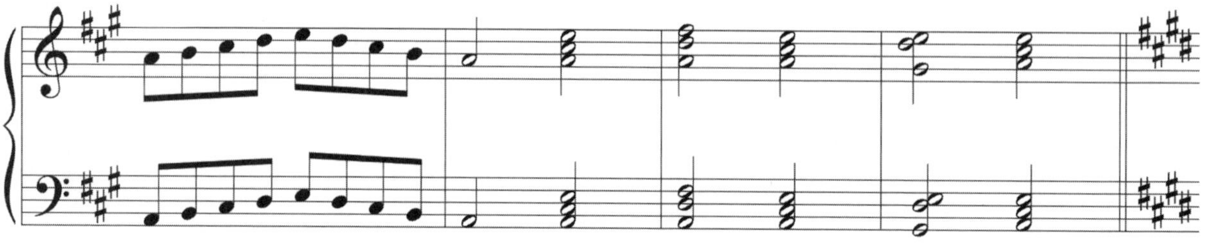

E MAJOR

B MAJOR

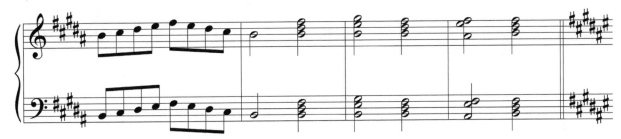

F# MAJOR (ENHARMONIC G♭)

G♭ MAJOR (ENHARMONIC F#)

C# MAJOR (ENHARMONIC D♭)

D♭ MAJOR (ENHARMONIC G♯)

A♭ MAJOR

E♭ MAJOR

B♭ MAJOR

F MAJOR

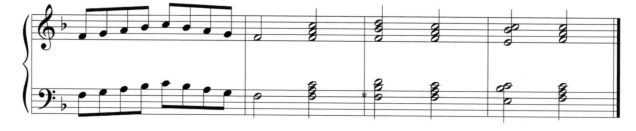

Minor 5-Finger Patterns and Primary Chord Progressions

A MINOR

E MINOR

B MINOR

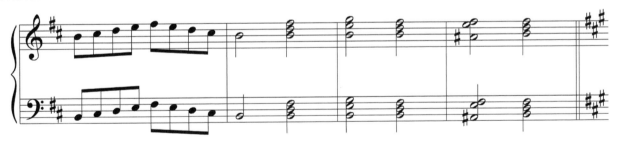

F♯ MINOR

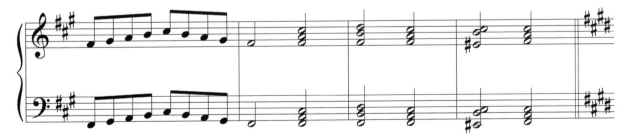

C♯ MINOR

G♯ MINOR (ENHARMONIC A♭)

DOUBLE SHARP

A♭ MINOR (ENHARMONIC G♯)

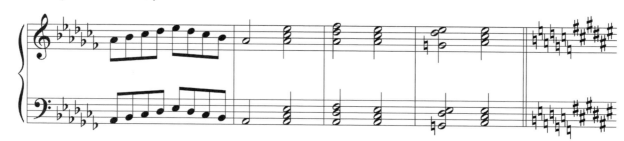

D♯ MINOR (ENHARMONIC E♭)

E♭ MINOR (ENHARMONIC D♯)

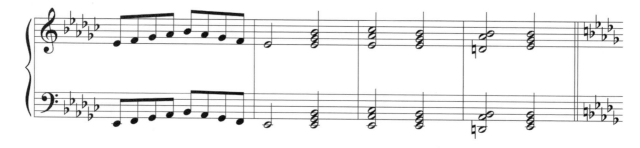

B♭ MINOR

F MINOR

C MINOR

G MINOR

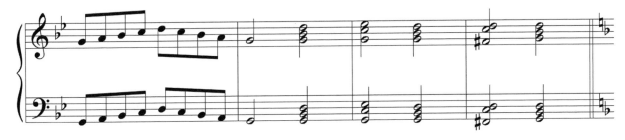

D MINOR

Major Scales

C MAJOR

G MAJOR

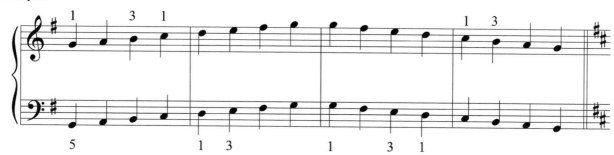

D MAJOR

A MAJOR

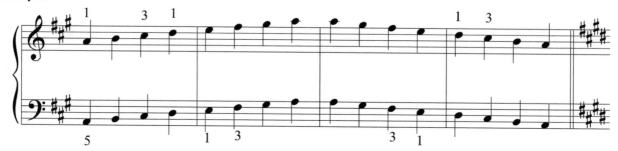

E MAJOR

B MAJOR

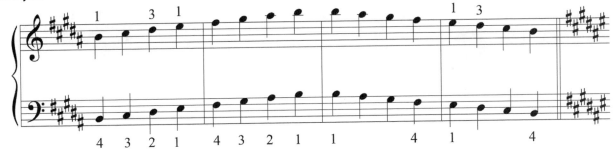

F# MAJOR (ENHARMONIC G♭)

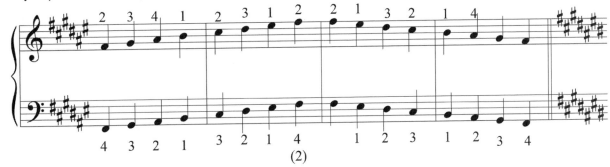

(2)

G♭ MAJOR (ENHARMONIC F#)

C# MAJOR (ENHARMONIC D♭)

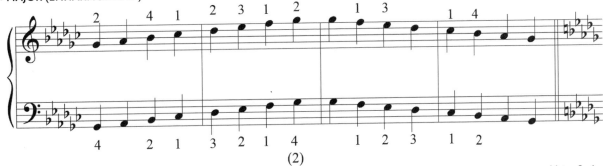

(2)

D♭ MAJOR (ENHARMONIC G♯)

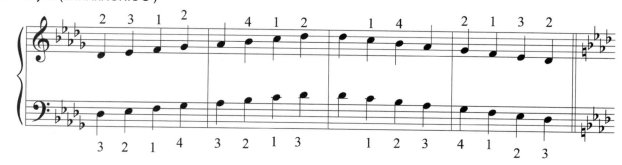

A♭ MAJOR

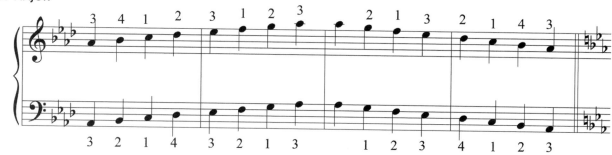

E♭ MAJOR

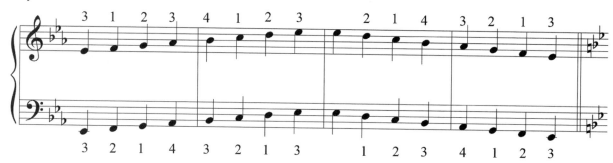

B♭ MAJOR

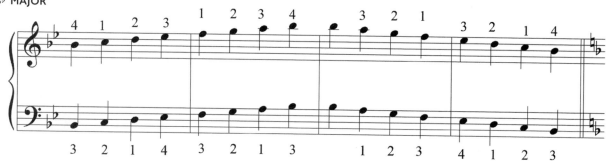

F MAJOR

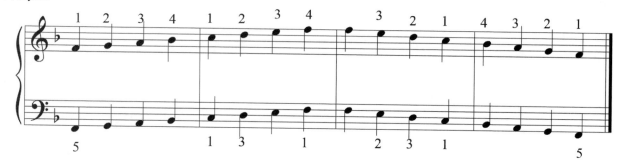

Selected Harmonic Minor Scales

A HARMONIC MINOR

E HARMONIC MINOR

B HARMONIC MINOR

C♯ HARMONIC MINOR

D HARMONIC MINOR

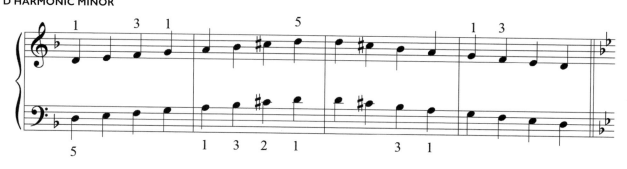

G HARMONIC MINOR

C HARMONIC MINOR

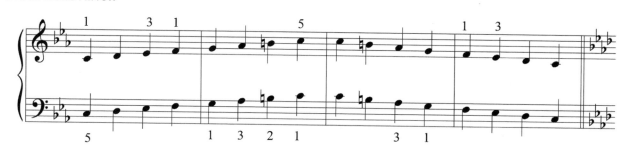

F HARMONIC MINOR

Two-Octave Arpeggios

Practice arpeggios with separate hands.

C MAJOR

G MAJOR

D MAJOR

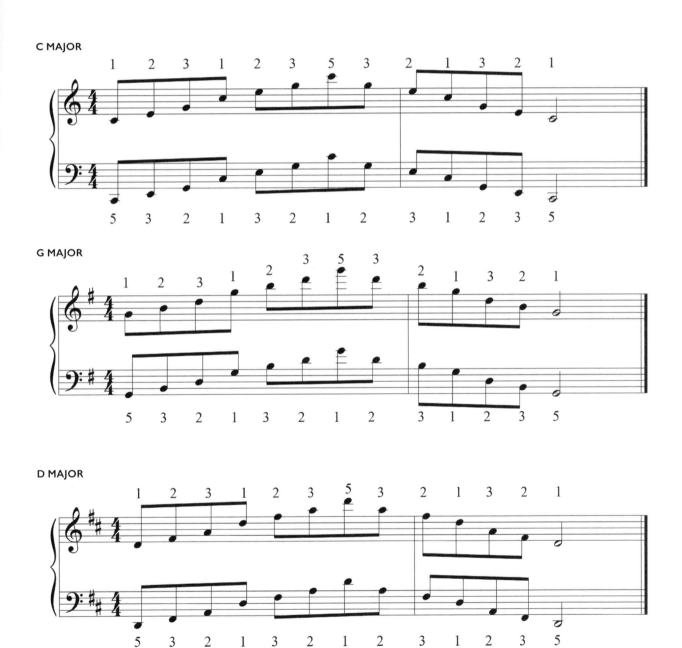

A MAJOR

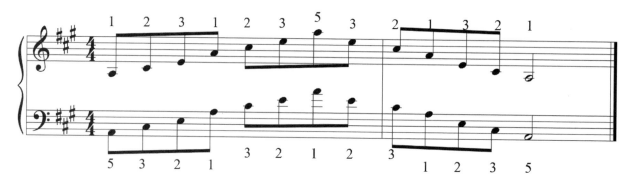

E MAJOR

B MAJOR

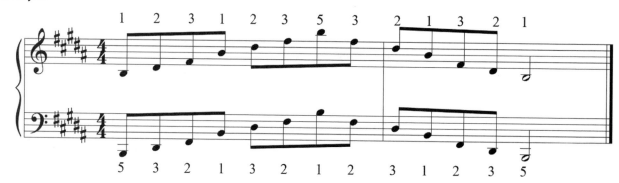

F♯ MAJOR (ENHARMONIC G♭)

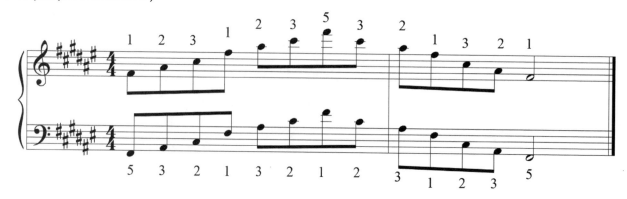

G♭ MAJOR (ENHARMONIC F♯)

C♯ MAJOR (ENHARMONIC D♭)

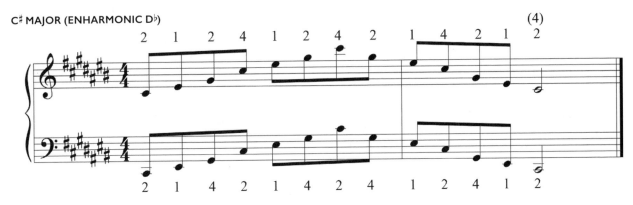

D♭ MAJOR (ENHARMONIC C♯)

A♭ MAJOR

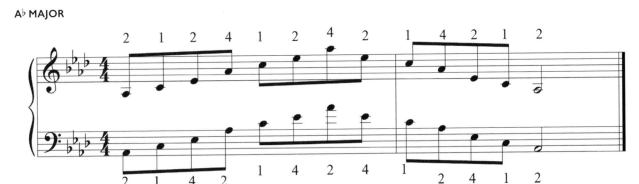

E♭ MAJOR

B♭ MAJOR

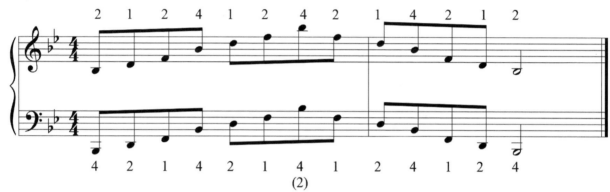

(2)

F MAJOR

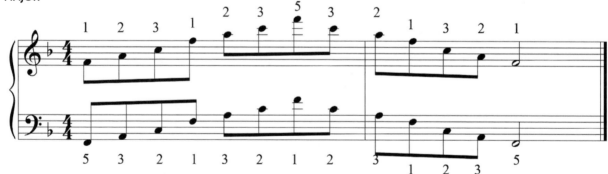

Index of Musical Repertoire

Bibliography

EXPERTISE AND DISCIPLINE

Ericsson, Anders, and Robert Pool. *Peak: Secrets from the New Science of Expertise.* Boston: Mariner Books, 2017.

Leonard, George. *Mastery: The Keys to Success and Long-Term Fulfillment.* New York: Plume, 1992.

LEISURE AND ADULT PIANO STUDY

Cooke, Charles. *Playing the Piano for Pleasure: The Classic Guide to Improving Skills through Practice and Discipline.* New York: Skyhorse Publishing, 2011.

Fay, Amy. *Music Study in Germany: The Classic Memoir of the Romantic Era.* Mineola, NY: Dover Publications Inc., 2011.

LIGHT-HEARTED MUSIC HISTORY

Barber, David W. *Bach, Beethoven, and the Boys: Music History as It Ought to Be Taught.* Toronto: Indent Publishing, 2014.

TECHNIQUE BOOKS

Palmer, Willard A., Morton Manus, and Amanda Vick Lethco. *The Complete Book of Scales, Chords, Arpeggios & Cadences.* Van Nuys, CA: Alfred Music Publishing Co, Inc., 1994.

Royal Conservatory of Music. *The Royal Conservatory of Music Piano Technique Book, 2008 Edition.* Toronto: Frederick Harris Music Co., Limited, 2008.

INTERNET RESOURCES

Music Teachers National Association. www.mtna.org.

"Find a Music Teacher." *Music Teachers National Association.* https://www.mtna.org/MTNA/Connect/Find_A_Teacher/MTNA/FindATeacherAddress.aspx?hkey=cd5d49b9-bb6e-486f-b643-1be7eb8bef4d.